Neglected Wells: Spirituality and the Arts

"Neglected Wells"

SPIRITUALITY AND THE ARTS

EDITED BY

Anne M. Murphy and Eoin G. Cassidy

FOUR COURTS PRESS

Set by Verbatim Typesetting & Design, Dublin,
in 11 on 13 Ehrhardt for
FOUR COURTS PRESS LTD
Kill Lane, Blackrock, Co. Dublin, Ireland
E-mail: fcp @ indigo.ie
and in North America for
FOUR COURTS PRESS
c/o ISBS, 5804 N.E. Hassalo Street, Portland, OR 97213.

A catalogue record for this title
is available from the British Library.

ISBN 1-85182-294-1

Printed in Ireland
by ColourBooks Ltd, Dublin.

Preface

Since the beginning of creation, when God saw that his handiwork was good, spirituality and creativity have been inextricably bound together. A belief in this connectedness is the thematic link which binds the essays included here under their unifying title: 'Spirituality and the Arts'.[1] In their range of subjects – from classical philosophies of beauty to Celtic scholarship, through the mysticism of Patrick Kavanagh and the witness of women's writing, and from the sacred sounds of Faure through the spiritual impact of the visual arts to the prophetic soundings of contemporary Irish writing – the essays offer a broad canvas of human, cultural and spiritual interest. The concerns of the contributors go beyond those of aesthetics and beyond historical or empirical analysis of specialist data. Areas of expertise in art, literature, history and music interface with philosophical and theological disciplines and intrigue both the mind and the spirit.

Human creativity is a reflection of divine creativity. Like divine creativity, it takes many forms and is expressed through many gifts. Human creativity, as the expression of hopes, needs and desires, witnesses to that instinct within the human spirit which energises women and men to see beyond the limitations of temporal existence and to rise above them. Human creativity is a statement of hope and a statement of belief that life is meaningful. The essays presented in this collection forcefully reiterate these statements. As testaments to human creativity, they articulate, in their investigation of sign and symbol, word and image, the human craving for permanence and value, a craving essentially for immortality.

The dialogue between faith and art is no new concept. Evidence from earliest civilisations and cultures bears witness to the cathartic and transcendent role of art in human attempts to express the emotional tensions related to the high points of living and dying – ultimately a religious context. The creative artist has always been at the forefront of the search for meaning and significance. It is perhaps the vocation of the artist to express this searching dimension of being human. The creative artist is the spokesperson, often unawares, whose art can offer to fellow human beings a perspective on the ultimate questions of life and death.

[1]This collection of essays derives in the main from a series of public lectures under the title 'Spirituality and the Arts', which was hosted by Mater Dei Institute of Education in 1995.

Through his or her giftedness, the artist becomes the prophet and visionary whose art proclaims and posits meaning, because art cannot escape, of its very nature, being significant. The imagination can indeed uncover neglected wells of revelation from which this collection draws.

Our century has experienced and continues to experience what might be described as a crisis of meaning. Yet there is much evidence in our contemporary society of a hunger for the spiritual. There is, for example, a growing interest in aspects of Eastern religions, such as yoga and transcendental meditation. The symphonic music of Gorecki has entered the category of best-sellers along with Tavener's hauntingly evocative The Protecting Veil, and there is the phenomenon of Gregorian chant sung by a choir of Spanish monks outselling pop titles. All of this suggests a yearning in the contemporary spirit for some kind of spiritual arc against the flood of meaninglessness which frequently threatens to engulf us. In our materialistic age, perhaps the arts offer to many the only accessible and acceptable doors to the transcendent or religious dimension of life.

The potential superficiality of contemporary living poses a particular challenge to the Christian. Christian educators have long believed passionately in the disclosive and transformative power of great art. Great art reveals something of the mystery and essential harmony of being human. Its transformative power discloses vestiges of that state of divine relatedness which constitutes humanness. It can suggest something of the meaning behind the often dissonant counterpoint of light and darkness created by life and death. But anyone who has ever been moved by picture, poem or symphony will understand that such an epiphany of hope and meaning is beyond immanent data and dogmatic proofs. It is a theophany transcending considerations of formal faith or culture. This experience is like that of Job who heard His 'songs in the night'. It is to touch the hem of the eternal.

These essays remind us that, with all our weakness, brokenness, guilt and shame, there is in our humanness a creative, shining spirit.

Anne M. Murphy, RSHM, PhD
Eoin G. Cassidy, DPh

Mater Dei Institute, August 1996

Contents

List of Illustrations

List of Contributors

UNA AGNEW, a St Louis Sister, is a lecturer in Spirituality at the Milltown Institute of Philosophy and Theology (Dublin). She has completed a doctoral thesis entitled 'The Word made Flesh: The Mystical Dimension of Patrick Kavanagh's Work' and lectures widely on this topic.

EOIN G. CASSIDY is a lecturer in Philosophy at Mater Dei Institute of Education in Dublin. He obtained his doctorate in Philosophy in 1990 from the Institut Superieur de Philosophie, Louvain, Belgium. He is a former treasurer of the Irish Philosophy Society and secretary of the Irish Theological Society.

JOHN DEVITT is Head of the English Department at Mater Dei Institute since 1979. He has published critical essays on Yeats, Kavanagh and Heaney and coedited the three-volume anthology *Bronze by Gold*.

EILEEN KANE is a Statutory Lecturer in the Department of the History of Art in University College Dublin. Her publications have mainly concentrated on art and patronage in Avignon and Rome in the fourteenth and fifteenth centuries.

MARGARET KELLEHER lectures in English at Mater Dei Institute. She is the author of *The Feminization of Famine: the Inexpressible Expressed*, a study of representations of women in famine literature (Cork University Press, 1996). She is co-editor (with James H. Murphy), of *Separate Spheres?: Gender and Nineteenth-Century Ireland*, forthcoming from Irish Academic Press.

MICHAEL MAHER MSC is lecturer in Scripture and coordinator of courses in Celtic Spirituality at Mater Dei Institute. He holds a PhD in Semitic Languages and has published widely on biblical and Jewish topics. He has contributed articles on different aspects of Celtic Spirituality to such journals as *Irish Theological Quarterly*, *Hallel*, and *Milltown Studies* and edited *Irish Spirituality* (Dublin, 1981).

ANNE M. MURPHY RSHM is Head of the Music Department at Mater Dei Institute. She is a musician and a theologian and her doctoral and post-doctoral research, on which she gained a Research Fellowship from Yale University, focuses on the dialogue between faith and the arts.

GESA THIESSEN is Associate Lecturer at the Milltown Institute of Theology and Philosophy. She is involved in interdisciplinary research between theology and art and has contributed articles to leading Irish theological journals.

Acknowledgements

We would like to thank the following, whose generosity assisted in making this publication possible:

Cardinal Cahal Daly DD, archbishop of Armagh
Most Rev. Desmond Connell DD, archbishop of Dublin
Most Rev. Laurence Forristal DD, bishop of Ossory
Fiachra O'Cellaigh DD, auxiliary bishop of Dublin
Noreen O'Carroll PhD
Ulster Bank Limited
Bank of Ireland Limited
Mater Dei Institute of Education
Vincentian Order, Irish Province
Sisters of St Louis, Irish Province
Avila, Carmelite Centre of Spirituality
Manresa House, Jesuit Centre of Spirituality
Missionaries of the Sacred Heart, Irish Province
Sisters of the Sacred Heart of Mary, Irish Province

Pathways to God:
Beauty, the Road Less Travelled

EOIN G. CASSIDY

The pathways to God have become less clearly marked, some might say, overgrown. Changes in European culture in recent years have brought many benefits, not least in terms of a positive response to the demands for the freedom of religious expression. Yet, paradoxically, there are few who would deny that access to the spiritual or transcendent dimension of life has become increasingly difficult to negotiate – even for adults who have been reared in one of the Christian traditions. I suggest that the aesthetic dimension of reality offers the contemporary secular society one of the very few points of contact with a world in which the spiritual can be appreciated. I am not denying the validity of the many other pathways to God generated by, for example, the dialogue between science and religion or among those engaged in the struggle for social liberation. However, I would argue that the experience of beauty and the mystery of artistic creation offers a privileged insight into that dimension of reality suggested by the idea of the spiritual.

This essay takes as its theme the value of the pathway to God suggested by the love of beauty. In the context of this study we will examine the cultural and historical reasons which make it today a road less travelled. It will be contended that, since the Enlightenment, subjectivist theories of beauty have progressively isolated aesthetic experience and its object, human creative endeavour, over against nature and being, and even moral character. This development has the effect of enclosing art in an artificial cocoon and, at the same time, denying beauty its proper transcendental status. The challenge facing those concerned to recover the link between beauty and religious experience is to recover the metaphysical dimension of aesthetic experience.

> Begin with the assumption that there exists an absolute Beauty, and an absolute Good ... It appears to me that if anything besides absolute Beauty is beautiful, it is so simply because it partakes of absolute beauty.[1]

This belief that there exists an absolute beauty was one which Plato never doubted. Not only in the *Phaedo* but also particularly in the *Symposium* and the *Phaedrus* one finds a most sensitively drawn and passionately expressed portrayal of human nature in terms of the quest for that which is beautiful. Alongside truth and goodness he both placed beauty at the apex of a hierarchical ordering of reality and proclaimed that it is the love of beauty as well as truth and goodness which defines human nature. It could be argued that something of this vision has marked culture since the dawn of civilisation. What is unquestionable is that the classical Greek culture, which gave birth to European civilisation as we know it, would be unimaginable shorn of its sensitivity to the existence and drawing power of beauty.

A SIGNPOST FOR AN INTELLIGIBLE WORLD

The world in which we live – is it intelligible? What are the pointers or signposts written on the face of the universe which allow us to assert the intelligibility of the cosmos? In the sixth century BC the classical world of Greek philosophy emerged in the form of a series of meditations on this theme. Among the earliest of these philosophers/religious thinkers were the Pythagoreans, a philosophical or religious community forever remembered for the symbol of the Tetracty which was used to affirm and explain the intelligibility of the universe. Based on a primitive analysis of musical notation which can be displayed in diagrammatic form, it reveals at a glance that the digit ten can be symbolised by a combination of the first four digits. More importantly, the Pythagoreans recognised that the chief musical intervals are expressible in simple numerical ratios between these first four digits, that is, an octave 2:1, a fifth 3:2 and a fourth 4:3.

According to tradition, the Tetracty was a sacred symbol for the universe, one that gave expression to the intuition that the universal experience of harmony is proof that the cosmos is intelligible. If the musical scale can be explained in terms of the imposition of definite proportions on the indefinite continuum of sound between high and low, might not the same principles underlie the whole universe? The experience of musical harmony and the existence of the science of mathematics did indeed prompt the Pythagoreans both to affirm the intelligibility of the universe and to propose principles which they believed governed the structures of the universe.

The startling nature of their insight is that the aesthetic motif of Beauty – the experience of proportion or harmony, expressed in music and analysed in terms of mathematical principles – pointed beyond the familiar or quotidian to a transcendent and divine source of meaning. It was an insight which the classical culture never lost and one which, has in no small measure, defined the Graeco-Roman civilisation. There is a continuous line which links Greece to Rome – one which stretches from Pythagoras to Plato, to the Neoplatonists and finally, to Augustine of Hippo. Linking all these is not only the conviction that the universe is intelligible but also the idea that Beauty is the foundational revelation of that which is divine – the One or God. Even though the status of beauty as one of the transcendentals alongside truth and goodness was the subject of dispute in the medieval world of Christendom, it is unquestionably the case that the link between the experience of beauty and the affirmation of a divine source of meaning has informed the history of European culture.

The historical line linking Greece to Rome acknowledges that the experience of beauty proclaims the intelligibility of the universe. It is one which asserts the link between the aesthetic and the ontological in terms of the motifs of unity/simplicity harmony or proportion/order. What is not often recognised is that this unity of perspective is replicated in the earliest quests to understand the mystery of Being in terms of the narrower focus imposed by the question of the meaning of human existence.

A PATHWAY TO GOD

Classical anthropology, which was born out of the Socratic command 'Know thyself!' responds to that inescapable question of whether human beings can ever be intelligible to themselves or to others. From Plato to Augustine the classical world never doubted that the answer to this question was to be found in terms of the mysterious attraction of the human soul for beauty. Not only the intelligibility of the universe but also the intelligibility of human life can be imaginatively intuited through the prism that is beauty.

> I was in love with beauty of a lower order and it was dragging me down. I used to ask my friends 'Do we love anything unless it is beautiful?' What, then, is beauty and in what does it consist? What is it that attracts us and wins us over to the things we love? Unless there were beauty and grace in them, they would be powerless to win our hearts.[2]

Human life was for Augustine as it was for Plotinus and Plato before him the drama of 'fall and return', 'descent and ascent', or 'sin and redemption'. What is common to all three philosophers is the conviction that life is lived in the light of the attractiveness of beauty, an attractiveness which has the power to destroy as well as to ennoble the human spirit.

For Augustine, the story of his autobiographical *Confessions* is the parable of the prodigal son seen through an aesthetic lens. He was acutely conscious that the journey to self-discovery is inseparable from that which seeks beauty and ultimately seeks God. But he never doubted that this journey was only possible because we are attracted by beauty – which to the eyes of Augustine has its source and completion in God, the one who is beautiful.

> I have learned to love you late, Beauty at once so ancient and so new! I have learned to love you late! You were within me, and I was in the world outside myself. I searched for you outside myself and, disfigured as I was, I fell upon the lovely things of your creation. You were with me but I was not with you.[3]

The drama of that epic struggle endured by the young Augustine – the struggle to find a home for his restless or homeless heart is one that informed many of the early Christian writings. It is a perspective in which the ethical character of our response to beauty is acknowledged. One can become ethically as well as aesthetically tone deaf or blind to the attraction of beauty. As Augustine recognised, beauty is not something which coerces us or denies human freedom. Furthermore, as the above quotation suggests, we are answerable for the manner in which we respond to the attraction of beauty, an attraction which, to the eyes of Augustine, was synonymous with the call of God.

The history of European art, music, poetry is one which up until quite recently continued to be a source of inspiration for those concerned to explore the link between beauty and religion. Who could imagine the creation of Chartres cathedral or Dante's *Divine Comedy* if they had no sensitivity to this classical world where the intelligibility of the world and human destiny was bound up with a sense of the divine presence in all things? Even as late as Blake, Keats and Coleridge[4] in the nineteenth century one can hear echoes of this classical vision.

> 'Beauty is truth, truth is beauty',
> – that is all
> Ye know on earth, and all ye need to know.[5]

Who, for example, could listen to Verdi's *Requiem* without becoming aware that the meaning of the composition is in some way bound up with religious inspiration! However, to the ears of his contemporaries this ready acceptance of a link between beauty and religion began to appear increasingly anachronistic.

BEAUTY IS IN THE EYE OF THE BEHOLDER

The first significant challenge to the classical world view came with the Enlightenment, that philosophical and cultural movement of the seventeenth and eighteenth century which ushered in the modernist era. The Scottish philosopher David Hume was the first to propose a detailed theory which called into question the objectivity of beauty, the link between the aesthetic and ontological and the identification of the love of beauty with the love of truth, goodness and God. According to Hume there is simply no such quality as beauty existing in objects outside the mind.

> To seek the real beauty, or real deformity, is as fruitless an inquiry, as to pretend to ascertain the real sweet or real bitter. According to the disposition of the organs, the same object may be both sweet and bitter.[6]

Beauty is something that exists in the mind which contemplates them. It is, or depends on, a feeling in the observer and will vary according to the dispositions of the person concerned. This subjectivist theory of beauty which contrasts sharply with the classical vision is one which was to have a major influence in terms of the development of twentieth century positivist/ empiricist and behaviourist aesthetic theory. Both of these philosophies would deny that there is any qualitative difference between human beings and any of the other species which inhabit the world. They would explain the idea and the attractiveness of beauty in terms of biological or social conditioning which is tied to the reproductive processes and designed to further the survival of the species.

Is something beautiful because it is desirable, pleasurable, or valuable, or is something desirable, pleasurable, or valuable because it is beautiful? With few exceptions, the classical world view is premised on the acceptance of the latter outlook. It is a view which is clearly at odds with the perspective of Hume, namely that beauty is simply a product of a subjective emotional state. Furthermore, this classical belief in the objective existence of beauty is not one which sits easily with the contemporary positivist/empiricist approach that is influenced by Hume and proposes an exclusively immanent and materialist world view. On the contrary, those who value this classical perspective would wish to argue that the experience of beauty reveals a transcendent and spiritual dimension to reality. Furthermore, they would contend that it is only possible to do justice to this experience if one acknowledges that a world bounded by the limits of empirical/scientific facts is not co-terminous with the real world. Rather, they would wish to argue that the experience of beauty points to something which underpins and transcends the world as perceived by the senses.

It seems increasingly difficult to argue in support of this classical viewpoint, because, in a contemporary culture influenced by empiricist presuppositions, evidence for the existence of anything is increasingly limited to the idea of scientific evidence. However, as is obvious, one will never discover the objective existence of beauty if one's search is limited to the strictly scientific or empirical analysis of that which can be seen through a microscope or at the end of a telescope. The search for beauty calls for a broader and more inclusive view both of what counts as a valid experience and how one defines the limits of human knowledge.

ART FOR ART'S SAKE

Another strand in the philosophical thought of the Enlightenment is to be found in the writings of the German philosopher Immanuel Kant.[7] His views were to have as profound an influence on the subsequent course of aesthetic theory as anything proposed by Hume. What Kant proclaims is not only the autonomy of beauty but also the subordination of beauty to art, the aesthetic object. It is a new vision of beauty freed from the cognitive, moral, and religious bonds that Kant claimed had constrained artistic creation. In opposition to the classical ideal which linked the love of beauty with the love of God, he proposed the ideal of a disinterested love of beauty and inaugurated an era which would take as its motto 'Art for art's sake'. It was this 'purist' ideal of disinterested artistic creation which was to define aesthetics in the modernist era and would increasingly influence the understanding of artistic creation up until the second half of the present century. In this vision beauty is at once shorn of any connection or subordination to truth and goodness and freed from religion: artistic creation should not be required to mean something or point to something, rather it should be allowed the freedom to be itself.

It is hard not to be sensitive to the value of this movement which placed such emphasis on allowing the purely aesthetic dimension of reality – the beauty of form – to stand apart. For too long the tendency had been to evaluate the artistic creation exclusively in terms of what it referred or pointed to. However, as a theory, this formalist or purist vision of art was not without its difficulties. In distancing beauty from either goodness or truth it contributed to the attempt to remove art from the wider human experience.[8]

Can one deny the distinctions which are made between an artist and a charlatan or between art and kitsch? It could be argued that the attempt to do so would only serve to aid those keen to manipulate the artistic community for propagandist purposes. Furthermore, is it possible to do justice to an artistic creation without acknowledging an ideal of perfection which art strives to realise?[9] The work of art restoration is a reminder of the different layers which underlie a finished product – layers which speak of a quest for perfection. Who does not admire the striving for perfection reflected in the many revisions of a poetic line or a musical score? The difference between a charlatan and an artist is that only the latter is preoccupied with this ideal. Has anyone ever heard, touched or laid eyes on the perfect sculpture, poem or musical score? Yet, who would deny that the ideal of the perfect is any less real for being transcendent? Who would deny that perfection, although always beyond reach is nevertheless desirable! In the relation between the artist and this ideal of perfection one can recognise an ethical and, indeed, a religious dimension to artistic creation. The classical Greek culture was founded on the identification of the beautiful and the good with the divine. In adverting to this universal desire for perfection one can recognise the validity of this insight. The blurring of this classical vision is one of the most enduring legacies of the culture of the Enlightenment.

DECORATIVE DIVERSIONS OR MEANINGFUL SYMBOLS

Can one evaluate art without acknowledging a larger context within which human beings live and work? The idea of 'Art for art's sake' would suggest that this is both possible and desirable. For example, in the burial chambers at Newgrange in Ireland and the caves at Lescaux in France one finds an abundance of highly abstract designs. From a purist or formalist perspective these must be evaluated purely in terms of their decorative or artistic merit. There would be no question of attempting to understand or evaluate them in the context of any possible ritual or religious connections with the values and beliefs which animated the life of the community. Alternatively, however, one could argue that these are not simply or even primarily decorative designs but are symbols which may reflect a religious intent – a community's conscious attempt to give expression in symbolic form to a belief in a horizon of meaning that transcended day-to-day preoccupations.[10] One might suggest that some of these designs could be interpreted as symbols associated with a divine presence or a belief in transcendence. While not wishing to minimise the danger of reading too much significance into a series of abstract symbols from a very different age and culture, is it reasonable, nevertheless, to assume in an *a priori* fashion that their significance was purely decorative? Whatever about the merits of this particular case, it is undoubtedly true that, the purist or formalist vision of art associated with modernism has led to a secularisation of aesthetics in which all religious meanings are deemed to be irrelevant to the task of understanding the significance of artistic creation.

THE MEANING OF ART IS IN THE PLAYING OF A GAME

A criticism of the formalist or purist vision of art constitutive of modernism from a very different perspective has arisen in the last thirty years with the emergence of post-modernism under the broad headings of structuralism and deconstructionist theory. Approaching a critical analysis of art from a variety of perspectives, that is, sociological, political, psycho-analytical, post-modernists place serious question marks over whether the ideal of 'Art for art's sake' was ever realised in practice or ever could be realised. Precise definitions of post-modernism are hard to come by, but post-modernists of a variety of hues would be united in suggesting that the idea of the aesthetic is a fiction, one fabricated for the most part by those concerned to promote privilege and power. This is particularly evident in those whose writings have been influenced by the neo-Marxist critique of art associated with the Frankfurt School and the structuralist Marxist movement in France.

One of the main exponents of deconstruction theory is the French philosopher Jacques Derrida. His writings offer a trenchant critique of the all-embracing theories of meaning which have largely defined the history of Western philosophy, and he proposes what is in essence an anti-aesthetic.[11] It is a theory which proclaims that there is no point of reference for art and that the idea of beauty is an ideological construct designed to offer the illusion of a world of meaning – the illusion of an intelligible universe. In this perspective it is not just beauty which is consigned to the world of fiction but equally truth, goodness, and ultimately God. To quote the contemporary philosopher and literary critic George Steiner:

> 'In the beginning was the Word.' There was no beginning, says deconstruction; only the play of sounds and markers amid the mutations of time.[12]

The classical Greek world whose influence is to be seen almost up the present speaks of a world of beauty which reveals the presence of the divine. It proclaims a world in which the experience of beauty admits one to the Logos, the Word, the revelation of God's presence. That is the premise upon which Western theology, metaphysics and aesthetics have been created. This vision has been described as a metaphysics of presence and it is precisely this premise of a metaphysics of presence that is denied by deconstructionist theory proposed by Jacques Derrida. In this sense, deconstruction offers us a forceful expression of contemporary nihilism

Without accepting the nihilism of deconstructionist theory one can have a certain sympathy for some elements of the post-modernist critique of classical and modernist aesthetics. For instance, one must recognise the effect of social, cultural and biological conditioning on both what is perceived as beautiful and what is deemed to be attractive in art. Similarly, while not wishing to accept the anarchic relativism of deconstruction it is important to be sensitive to the subjective dimension in the evaluation of artistic creation which gives rise to the well worn phrase 'There is no accounting for taste.' Furthermore, one does not have to be a particularly diligent student of contemporary history to recognise the way in which art in all it forms can be used to further ideological or propagandist goals. Incidentally, anyone who reads the writings of such classical authors as Plato or Augustine could not be unmindful of their awareness of the potentiality of artistic creation to distort beauty as much as to reveal it.

Are we to accept alongside empiricists and behaviourists that an idea of beauty transcending the boundaries of a scientific world is literally non-sense,[13] or that beauty is to be explained simply in terms of biological or social conditioning tied to the reproductive process and designed to further the survival of the species? Are we to accept the views of post-modernists that artistic creation is either to be explained as a therapeutic act to assist one to cope with unresolved conflicts or that the significance of art is akin to the meaning which we attach to the playing of a game?

While one can accept that there is a certain validity to the post-modernist critique of classical and modern culture, nevertheless, the idea of the artist as *homo ludens* is not one to which many would easily subscribe. Similarly, the idea expounded by behaviourism and positivist/empiricist philosophy, that beauty can be explained exclusively in terms of psychological theory such as subjective feeling linked to biological or social conditioning, is one which many would regard as excessively reductionist.[14] However, the question remains as to whether there exists a viable alternative to these views and one which offers a credible account of beauty and artistic creation in terms of a theistic world view. The challenge facing those concerned to recover the link between beauty and religious experience is to offer a theory of beauty and artistic creation which counters:

1   The empiricist/positivist viewpoint which proclaims that the existence of an objectively real standard of beauty transcending the material or scientific world is literally non-sense, and that the experience of beauty can be explained in terms of subjective feeling;

2   Scepticism or agnosticism in regard to the objective existence of beauty which underpins a contemporary consumerist or pragmatic approach to the evaluation of art;

3   The nihilism inherent in much of what is called post-modernism and which is expressed in the view that all art is play designed in no small measure to underline the absurdity of seeking meaning where there is none to be found.

AN INTIMATION OF RESTLESSNESS AND HOMELESSNESS

Where then can one look to find evidence for the objective existence of beauty which resists the criticisms outlined above? An unusual starting point, but one which may ultimately prove fruitful, is to examine the way in which we react to the experiences of disunity, conflict, or the lack of harmony which tragically mark so much of human existence. There is no one who at some level of their existence is either unaware of or at ease with these experiences. They force us to acknowledge that the world as it is experienced is in some sense a 'broken world'.

The phrase 'a broken world' is taken from the writings of the twenti-eth-century French philosopher Gabriel Marcel.[15] Conscious of the uni-versality of that experience he reflected on what living in a broken world informs us about human nature and the way in which human beings perceive their relationship to the world. It struck him that it is only pos-sible to place the experience of disunity or conflict under the rubric of a broken world if one has both an intuition of, and a desire for, an alter-native world – one marked by the values of unity and harmony which, incidentally, are the very motifs which we identify with beauty.

From where do we obtain this intuition of a harmonious world and what prompts us to desire the goal of unity? The experience of restless-ness or homelessness suggested by the phrase 'a broken world' raises in no uncertain terms the question of whether or not there exists a tran-scendent dimension to life. Are we to say that the intuition of beauty and the desire for a world touched by beauty is simply an illusory human projection or an ideological construct? Is beauty to be explained in terms of an elaborate attempt to cloak the absurdity of the world with a veneer of meaning – 'a type of patch-work quilt which warms and protects us from the chill winds of reality'? One could equally argue that the reverse is true and that those who would deny the existence of a spiritual and transcendent dimension to life are arbitrarily refusing to acknowledge the implications of the experience of homelessness or exile in a world from which beauty is absent.

REAL PRESENCES: FACT OR FICTION?

One does not have to accept a post-modernist perspective to be wary of insisting on too close a link between beauty and art. Anyone familiar with the writings of Plato or Augustine and even the iconoclast contro-versies in the Orthodox Churches would be aware of the complex nature of the dialogue generated by art and beauty. Nevertheless, it is not pos-sible to do justice to a study of the motif of beauty without examining the dialectic generated by the relationship between the acts of artistic creation and the reception or acceptance of a work of art. In a penetrat-ing critique of post-modernism, George Steiner offers us in his book *Real Presences* an enlightening treatment of this theme. In contrast to contemporary post-modernism the classical culture was, as we have seen, ever sensitive to an ethical and/or religious dimension to the acceptance of art and the longing for beauty. Steiner acknowledges the validity of this perspective in a penetrating analysis of the way in which we receive works of art. However, the particular merit of Steiner's analysis for the purposes of this article is that he offers a detailed and incisive treatment of the nature of artistic creation. It is a study which calls into question in no uncertain terms the post-modernist thesis that seeking meaning in beauty and the acts of artistic creation is akin to looking for reassurance in a desert from a mirage.

Is the artist one who offers us imperfect copies of what we see or hear, or one who alters reality for the purpose of propaganda? The former perspective reflects the context for the prejudice of Plato against the artist; the latter perspective is suggested in much of the writings of deconstructionists. But argues Steiner, can anyone who has studied the self-portraits of a painter like Van Gogh even for a moment presume that he was interested simply or even primarily in pictorial likeness, or is it credible that the self-portraits are altered simply for ideological reasons?

How do we explain the creation of a work of art? Steiner alerts us to the importance of the word 'creation' and points to the fact that anyone who has arranged flowers, written a poem, a novel or a play, anyone who has attempted even the simplest musical composition will recognise the creative impulse that lies at the heart of such endeavours.[16] What is it – this creative impulse? It is clearly linked to the desire to give birth to something new or unique, the desire to offer a new perspective, or the desire to reveal what has been hidden in the depths of one's own psyche.

The philosophical issue here touches on questions which defines us as human beings. As the twentieth-century German philosopher Martin Heidegger recognised, there is a question which is inescapable, one which defines us – that which asks, 'Why are there essents rather than nothing?'[17] The same question is suggested when one reflects on the mystery of human creation. Why is there beauty rather than banality, or why is there artistic creation rather than mere technological efficiency? The motif of beauty and artistic creation puts us in touch with the fundamental question of existence, that is, creation.[18]

Is the artist to be compared to one who wishes to be God, one who wishes to grasp the ultimate power to create out of nothing, one who can be likened to the classical figures of Prometheus and Sisyphus, or to the more contemporary figure of Nietzsche who challenged the power of the Gods? Or is the artist to be compared to a Christ figure – one who emptied himself in order to attend to, or to love, that which is other than himself? Has the creative impulse its origins in the desire to express one's power to create oneself and one's world, or does it have its origins in the desire to give recognition to that which is other than oneself? One's answers to this series of questions will largely depend upon whether one does or does not accept a theistic world view. However, in terms of the contemporary challenge to recover the classical links between art and religion, the idea of the artist as one who imitates or bears a trace of the divine artist is not one which ought to be dismissed lightly. It suggests that the artist can be understood as one who shares in, or images, the creative work of a loving God. In this perspective the artist is literally a co-creator with God.[19]

A WAGER ON TRANSCENDENCE

When reflecting on the link between art and creation there is another factor which needs to be acknowledged i.e. the irreducible otherness of a work of art. There are few who would deny that with every thing that becomes sayable in and through artistic creation there is as much again that remains unsayable or concealed. Steiner perceptively reminds us that art 'will never totally lose its strangeness, its otherness, its transcendence. Art never fully succeeds in naming or in taming that which is – Being'.[20]

In the same vein, Beauty is not something which can either be possessed or controlled by art. In this context, art speaks to us of the mystery of creation and reminds us of the dialectical relationship between that which is unconcealed or immanent and that which is concealed or transcendent.

In the last analysis when one reflects on the mystery of artistic creation there is a choice. Either one accepts that the world is absurd and that art is really playing at being God in a world without God – or simply playing. Alternatively, like Plato, Augustine, and more recently, Steiner, one places a wager on transcendence, a fundamental and defining trust that there is nevertheless a meaning – a presence.[21] The whole history of western civilisation up until very recently has been premised on this latter position. It is one which recognises that God and Beauty are ultimately indistinguishable and that the artist who is sensitive to the transcendence as well as the immanence of beauty has the potential to uncover what one might describe as the footprints of God in the universe.

THE DESIRE FOR IMMORTALITY

No treatment of artistic creation would be complete without an inquiry as to why so much of art takes the form of a celebration of the those moments in life which touch on the phenomena of birth and death. Perhaps, it is after all not so surprising that art records the drama of life and death, because there are few who would deny that human life is at some level lived in the light of the dialectic created by the transitoriness of life and the desire for immortality. It is not possible to ignore the truth expressed by Heidegger that 'as soon as one is born one is old enough to die'.[22] In this context, it is not surprising that much of art takes the form of a meditation on life lived in the shadow of death. Seen in this perspective, the mystery of artistic creation has the potential to evoke questions which touch on the spiritual, because all humans share with each other a sense of what Augustine calls 'the madness of loving that which is transitory'.[23]

The idea that artistic creation can offer us a glimpse of immortality is reflected in the following passage from the pen of W.B. Yeats:

> No man can create as did Shakespeare, Homer, Sophocles, who does not believe with all his blood and nerve, that man's soul is immortal, for the evidence lies plain to all men that where that belief has declined, men have turned from creation to photography.[24]

A reading of the classic treatment of beauty in Plato's *Symposium* reminds us that this idea is not new. The *Symposium* contains a sustained reflection on beauty in the context of the longing for immortality and the desire to create that which is immortal. According to Plato, love or eros, that quality which defines human nature, desires to touch or give expression to that which is immortal. In this context, we are all lovers of beauty, and artistic creation may be understood literally as an act which seeks to bring to birth that which possesses beauty and is marked by the stamp of immortality.

In summary, I have suggested that an analysis of the mystery of artistic creation has the potential to give us access both to the mystery of God's existence and to the spiritual dimension of human existence. It recognises that human beings are defined in terms of:

1 The desire to create or to give expression to that which is other than oneself – an insight which offers us the potential to see ourselves under the rubric of 'imago Dei'.

2 The desire to uncover the footprints of God in the world – a desire which nevertheless recognises, through the experience of the irre-

ducible otherness and transcendence of art, the truth that God can never be completely identified with the world as it is experienced.

3 The desire to affirm that decay and death do not constitute the ultimate horizons within which human existence is lived – an insight which situates art in the context of the longing to create that which is marked by a trace of eternity.

CONCLUSION

The thesis proposed in this essay is that the loss of the classical horizon in modern and post-modern aesthetics is a real loss in that it has contributed to the formation of a culture which has severed the links that connected art with spirituality, and beauty with God. This article has suggested, to the contrary however, that there are grounds to believe that the aesthetic dimension of experience will never lose its power to evoke an awareness of the spiritual. In this context, the longing for beauty has the possibility of offering us a unique insight into the religious dimension of human existence. Beauty is indeed a privileged pathway to God.

NOTES

1 Plato, *The Phaedo* 100, C, trans. H.N. Fowler (London, 1914), p. 345.
2 Augustine, *Confessions* IV, 13, trans. R.S. Pine Coffin (New York, 1961), p. 83. For a detailed treatment of the theme of beauty in the writings of Augustine, see Eoin G. Cassidy, 'Friendship and Beauty in Augustine' in F. O'Rourke (ed.), *At the Heart of the Real*, (Dublin, 1992), pp. 51-66.
3 Augustine, op. cit., pp. 231-2.
4 In Coleridge's sustained reflections on the nature of the poetic he acknowledges the importance of the links between the world of poetic imagination and that of truth. See George Watson (ed.), *Samuel Taylor Coleridge. Biographia Literaria* (London, 1965), chs. 13 and 14, esp. pp. 168-74
5 John Keats, 'Ode on a Grecian Urn', in Helen Vendler (ed.), *The Odes of John Keats* (London, 1983), p. 115.
6 David Hume, 'The Sceptic', in W.J. Lenz's edition of his essays (New York, 1965), p.6.

7 For a good introduction to the aesthetic theory of Immanuel Kant see Ingrid Stadler, 'Perception and Perfection in Kant's Aesthetics', and Robert L. Zimmerman, 'Kant: The Aesthetic Judgment', in Robert P. Wolff (ed.), *Modern Studies in Philosophy: Kant* (New York, 1967), pp. 339-84 and 385-408.

8 The difficulty of sustaining such a purist position can be seen in Keats's use of the phrase 'negative capability'. While stressing the importance of relishing possibility without any premature insistence on moral or philosophical certainty, the phrase, 'negative capability', suggests, nevertheless, an awareness of the larger horizon of human experience within which art must be situated. See Keats's letter to George and Thomas Keats (21 and 27 December, 1817), *Letters of John Keats*, edited by Robert Gittings (London, 1975), p. 43.

9 For a detailed treatment of this issue see the writings of the philosopher Iris Murdoch. In particular see *The Sovereignty of Good*, 1970, pp. 59-76; *Metaphysics as a Guide to Morals*, 1992, pp. 1-24 and 80-90; and *The Fire and the Sun: Why Plato Banished the Artists*, 1977.

10 See Brendan Purcell, 'In Search of Newgrange: Long Night's Journey into Day', in *Crane Bag*, vol. 2, no. 1 (Dublin, 1982), pp. 237-44.

11 For a general introduction to the aesthetic theory of Post-Modernism see Stuart Sim, 'Structuralism and post-structuralism' in Oswald Hanfling (ed.), *Philosophical Aesthetics: An Introduction* (Oxford, 1992), pp. 405-39. For a study of Derrida on this theme see Jacques Derrida, *Writing and Difference*, trans. Alan Bass (London, 1978), pp.3-30 and 278-93.

12 George Steiner, *Real Presences*, (London, 1989), p. 120.

13 The classic critique of this empiricist/positivist perspective is to be found in Ludwig Wittgenstein, *Tractatus Logico-Philosphicus*, trans. D.F. Pears and B.F. McGuinness (London, 1961), pp. 71-4.

14 In an impressive article Hugh Bredin remarks that the various psychological theories of art are 'singularly incapable of explaining aesthetic experience, of art and nature alike. Beauty is the only concept which appears to bestow upon art a place amid the furniture of the universe, to humanise it and overcome its growing alienation from our lives.' 'The Theory of Beauty' in James McEvoy (ed.), *Philosophy and Totality* (Belfast, 1977), p. 35.

15 For a good introduction to the philosophy of Gabriel Marcel see Kenneth T. Gallagher, *The Philosophy of Gabriel Marcel* (New York, 1975). The theme of the 'broken world' is to be found throughout the works of Marcel; in particular see Marcel, *Homo Viator*, trans. Emma Crauford (Chicago, 1951).

16 See Steiner, op. cit., pp. 200-10.

17 Martin Heidegger, *Introduction to Metaphysics*, trans. Ralf Manheim (New York, 1961), p. 1. For a detailed treatment of the importance of this issue see the chapter entitled 'The Fundamental Question', ibid, pp. 1-42.

18 I am idebted to my colleague John Devitt for alerting me to the passage in D.H. Lawrence's novel *The Rainbow* where Tom Brangwen responds to the beauty of the night sky with the insight that 'he did not belong to himself'; see D.H. Lawrence, *The Rainbow* (London, 1961), p. 40.

19 See Samuel Coleridge, *Biographia Literaria* (London, 1965), chs. 4, 13, and 14.

20 See Steiner op. cit., pp. 210-16.

21 Cf. ibid., pp. 214.

22 Heidegger's classic treatment of this theme is to be found in Martin Heidegger, *Being and Time*, trans. John Macquarrie and Edward Robinson (Oxford, 1973), pp. 279-311.

23 Augustine, *Confessions* IV, 7, trans. R.S. Pine Coffin (1961), p. 78.

24 W.B. Yeats. This is an extract from an unsigned article in the review *To-Morrow* which Richard Ellman has identified as having been written by Yeats: see Richard Ellman, *The Man and the Masks* (London, 1954), p. 250.

Saints and Scholars: Love of Learning in the Early Irish Church

MICHAEL MAHER MSC

When St Patrick arrived in Ireland he found, not a united kingdom governed by a single high king, but a large number of autonomous kingdoms that were ruled over by local kings or tribal chieftains who each ruled his territory with relative independence.[1] Although the society which Patrick got to know was non-literate[2] it was rich in oral tradition which was preserved, developed and handed on by a learned priestly caste that enjoyed considerable privileges and that was held in high esteem by contemporary society. This learned class mastered mythology, magic[3] and ritual, preserved historical and genealogical traditions which were recited on suitable occasions, and maintained a large body of law which was applied to society in general.

We can say very little with certainty about the conversion of Ireland to Christianity, and we are poorly informed about the relationship between the Christian Church and the learned elite in the fifth and sixth centuries. But by the seventh century the secular learned class had lost its priestly character and survived in the *fili* who cultivated historical tradition, and in the *brithem* who maintained the legal tradition and applied it to the lives of the people. The new ideas which the Christians brought to Ireland did not drown the old native learning. In fact, the Church assimilated the traditional secular learning and used it as a vehicle for the advancement of its own purposes, and by about the year 600 Ireland was well on the way to developing its own Christian culture.[4]

Nevertheless, the process of assimilation may not have been easy, and the legend that at the Convention of Druim Ceit in 575 Colm Cille saved the *fili* from banishment from Ireland may reflect a situation where the *fili* with their pagan lore were faced with the threat of expulsion. It may be noted however that the legend makes the point that although Colm Cille gave his support to the *fili* he also took the sting from their poems and set their minds on 'saying goodness', 'for until that time they had been wont to do folk to death with their satire'.[5] Some of the *fili* had their reservations about entering the clerical state as we gather from the preface to the Old Irish poem known as *Fiacc's Hymn*. This text, which was probably composed in the eighth century, shows the reluctance of Fiacc, the disciple of Dubthach, 'chief poet of Ireland', to accept Patrick's invitation to join the ranks of the clergy. Patrick, we are told, asked Dubthach to introduce him to a suitable candidate for Holy Orders. Dubthach nominated his pupil Fiacc, and the story continues as follows:

> 'How will it be,' said Patrick, 'if what we have been saying is not pleasing to him [to Fiacc]?' 'Proceed to tonsure me,' said Dubthach, 'so that he may see.' So when Fiacc saw that he asked: 'What is being proceeded with?' said he. 'To tonsure Dubthach' said they. 'That is idle,' said he, 'for there is not in Ireland a poet his equal.' 'You would be taken in his stead?' said Patrick. 'The loss of me,' said Fiacc, 'is less to Ireland than Dubthach.' So Patrick shore his beard from Fiacc then.[6]

Fiacc's response to Patrick's invitation can hardly be called enthusiastic, and he only agreed to become a cleric when he saw that his esteemed master was about to be tonsured. One must note that Fiacc's conviction that Dubthach's entry into the clerical state would be a loss for Ireland implies a negative view of the role of clerics as *fili*.

However, the Christianisation of the country advanced steadily in the fifth and sixth centuries, and the author of the *Félire Oengusso*, writing about the year 800, celebrated in triumphalist tones the victory of the Christian faith over paganism. The ancient strongholds of the pagan kings were, he proclaimed, in ruins while the monastic settlements flourished. Tara, Cruachan (the site of the kings of Connacht in Co. Roscommon), Emain Macha (the site of the kings of Ulster, near Armagh) and Aillenn (a fort in Co. Kildare) were all uninhabited, while the monasteries of Armagh, Clonmacnoise, Kildare and Glendalough were hives of activity where choirs of monks sang their melodious hymns.

> The old cities of the pagans ...
> They are waste without worship.
> The cells that have been taken by pairs and trios,
> They are Romes with multitudes, with hundreds, with thousands.
> Heathendom has been destroyed,
> Though fair it was and wide-spread;
> The Kingdom of God the Father
> Has filled heaven, earth and sea.[7]

It is very likely, however, that the victory of Christianity was not as

complete as this and other ecclesiastical texts might claim, and indeed
there are indications that even in the ninth century pagan beliefs and
practices were not altogether eliminated from the country.[8]

WRITING

When the Christians brought the Latin script to Ireland the native
scholars quickly adopted it for the writing of both Latin and Irish. They
soon developed their own style of writing, the so-called 'insular script',
which was to serve for the writing of Irish down to the middle of the
present century. It had thus the honour of being the longest-lived script
in Western Europe. Writing is, of course, not just a medium for communicating the thoughts of human minds or for recording the achievement of the generations. It is an art in itself, and in Ireland scribes and
artists of unsurpassed skill and ingenuity devoted themselves to the task
of producing books that have merited a place not only in the history of
medieval book-production but also in the history of art.

The Gospel Books in particular attracted the attention of scribes and
artists who not only wrote the sacred text in an elaborate script but also
added ornamentation of different kinds, portraits, decorative lettering,
stylized animal figures and abstract drawings. This elaborate decoration
or 'illuminaton' of the Gospel Books was intended as a sign of reverence
for the word of God. But at a time when there were no chapter or verse
divisions of the Bible the illuminated pages also had a practical purpose
since they helped the reader to find his or her bearing in the biblical
text.

Writing between 1185 and 1188 Giraldus Cambrensis or Gerald of
Wales, who did not always have flattering things to say about Ireland
and the Irish, describes the Gospel Book which he saw in Kildare as follows:

> Among all the miracles of Kildare nothing seems to me more
> miraculous than that wonderful book which they say was written
> at the dictation of an angel during the lifetime of the virgin
> [Brigid].
> This book contains the concordance of the Four Gospels accord-
> ing to St Jerome, with almost as many drawings as pages, and all
> of them in marvellous colours. Here you can look upon the face of
> the divine majesty drawn in a miraculous way; here too upon the
> mystical representations of the Evangelists, now having six, now

four, and now two wings. Here you will see the eagle; there the calf. Here the face of a man; there that of a lion. And there are almost innumerable other drawings. If you look at them carelessly and casually and not too closely, you may judge them to be mere daubs rather than careful compositions. You will see nothing subtle where everything is subtle. But if you take the trouble to look very closely, and penetrate with your eyes to the secrets of the artistry, you will notice such intricacies, so delicate and subtle, so close together and well-knitted, so involved and bound together, and so fresh still in their colourings that you will not hesitate to declare that all these things must have been the result of the work, not of men, but of angels.[9]

This description fits the *Book of Kells*, and it is often suggested that this is the book that was being described by Giraldus. It is more likely, however, that the book he saw belonged to Kildare and has long since disappeared.

SCRIBES AND SCRIPTORIA

Since Christianity is a religion of the book an inevitable consequence of the establishment of that religion in Ireland was the development of the art of transcribing manuscripts and producing books. The oldest surviving Irish manuscript, the *Cathach*, a copy of the Psalms which dates from about the year 600 and which is preserved in the Royal Irish Academy, and by the time the Book of Durrow was written sometime after 664 the art of book production and book illumination had reached a high degree of development.[10]

In the introduction to a collection of Irish ecclesiastical laws which were put together in the first half of the eighth century the compiler referred to the 'vast forest of writings' (*de ingenti silva scriptorum*) from which he had selected the documents which he put together.[11] Writing about the year 800 the author of the *Félire Oengusso* could refer to 'Ireland's hosts of books' which he had consulted in the preparation of his own work.[12] Even before 800 the fame of the Irish books had spread abroad as we know from a certain Aethichus Ister, who wrote on the continent some time between the sixth and the eighth centuries, and who claimed to have spent some time among the Irish 'examining their books' (*eorum volumina volvens*).[13] However, a note in *Lebor na hUidre* or the Book of the Dun Cow, shows that some of these books could disappear and that the libraries of ancient monasteries, like their modern counterparts, had to take the possibility of book-pilfering into account. The note describes the activity of a certain Flann Mainistrech (d. 1056) as follows:

> Flann then and Eochaid the Wise Ua Céirín gathered this material from the books of Eochaid Ua Flannacán in Armagh and from the books of Monasterboice and other choice books besides, namely, from the Yellow Book which is missing from the strong-room in Armagh, and from the Short Book of Monasterboice and that is the one which the student stole and brought with him overseas and which was never found again.[14]

However, we know very little about the scriptoria in which books were being produced in the sixth and seventh centuries and we know nothing at all about the scribes and artists who worked in these scriptoria. By the eighth century many monasteries had acquired considerable wealth and could afford the huge expenses which the maintenance of a scriptorium involved. The production of vellum or parchment alone would impose a heavy financial burden on a monastery. It has been estimated, for example, that about sixteen animals would be required for the production of a relatively small book like the Cathach, to which we have already referred. *Lebor na hUidre* or the Book of the Dun Cow, which we have also mentioned and which was written before 1106, is the oldest surviving manuscript written entirely in Irish. It is one of those 'one-volume libraries' or composite books that contained a collection of literary pieces of very different kinds, and it is said that as many as sixty animals would have been required for the original manuscript.[15] This statistic should be enough to give the lie to the legend that the Book of the Dun Cow was made from the hide of the cow which belonged to Ciaran, the founder of the monastery of Clonmacnoise where the book was written.

The great Annals like the Annals of Inisfallen, the Annals of Ulster, and the Annals of the Four Masters record the deaths of scribes from such monasteries as Derry, Kildare, Armagh, Bangor, Clonmacnoise, Clonard and Glendalough. The fact that scribes merited mention in the Annals is indicative of their importance and prestige, and it is very probable that only the head of a scriptorium, and not every copyist, was considered worthy of an annalistic obituary.[16]

We know from the manuscripts that survive that Irish scribes developed their own style and distinguished themselves from their continental counterparts in nearly every aspect of book production. They had their own particular way of preparing vellum and parchment from the hides of animals; they had their own method of ruling the pages; they had their own way of joining the pages within a book; they had their own abbreviations; and, of course, they had their own style of decoration and illumination. Wherever the Irish monks went they brought with them their books and their book-craft, and many books that were produced in Ireland or by Irish scribes on the continent are still to be found scattered throughout the libraries of Europe.

TO ENRICH THE MEN OF ART

One can conclude that the scribes took pride in their craft and realised its importance from the fact that so many of them signed their work, often adding invocations or requests for prayers. Thus, for example, the Irish scribe of the *Commentary on the Psalms*, which probably dates from the early ninth century and which is now in the Ambrosian Library in Milan, signs off as follows: *Diarmait scripsit: orate pro illo peccatore*, 'Diarmait wrote this: pray for that sinner.' The writer of the text of St John's Gospel which forms part of the Stowe Missal (*c*.800) signed his name in Ogham and completed his work with these words:

> I give thanks to God. Amen. It is finished. Amen. I ask whoever reads this book to remember me, the writer, a sinner, namely, Sonid, the pilgrim. May he be well who has written, and he for whom it has been written. Amen.

But it was not only when finishing his text that the scribe gave expression to his feelings, and many are the personal remarks that have been added on the margins of manuscripts by weary or distracted scribes.

The ninth-century Irish copyist of a Latin grammar now in St Gall in Switzerland frequently addresses a short prayer to the Trinity, to Christ, to Brigid, to Patrick, or to Diarmait. On one occasion he asks Patrick and Brigid to pray that a certain Mael Brigte (perhaps a master-scribe) might not be angry with him 'for the writing that has been written this time'. At other times he complains for various reasons. He writes, 'It's dark here'; 'Alas! my hand'; 'Oh my breast! Holy Virgin'; 'the parchment is rough, and the writing'; 'new parchment, bad ink. Oh, I say nothing more'; 'The ink is thin'.[17] Some of the monks who may have had to work hard in the fields or in the kitchen may have looked on the position of scribe as something of a sinecure. The scribes occasionally reacted to this attitude by adding marginal notes to the effect that the art of writing and transcribing was in fact very taxing and made great demands on the scribe. The eighth-century Irish writer of a manuscript which is now in Würzburg expressed his opinion on the matter in the following succinct comment: 'Three fingers may do the writing, but the whole body is involved in the work.'

In a relaxed mood a writer adds the following lines which are frequently printed in collections of old Irish poetry:

> A hedge of trees overlooks me; a blackbird's lay sings to me (an announcement which I shall not conceal); above my lined book the birds' chanting sings to me.
>
> A clear voiced cuckoo sings to me (goodly utterance) in a grey cloak from bush fortresses. The Lord is indeed good to me: well do I write beneath a forest of woodland.[18]

The *Leabhar Breac*, the largest surviving manuscript in the hand of one scribe and almost all in Irish, was written in north Tipperary in the first decade of the fifteenth century. The scribe frequently abandoned his main task to add prayers and comments on the margins of his text. The most common is 'A Mhuire fóir', 'Mary help'. On occasions when he was in a particularly bad mood he wrote remarks such as the following: I am weary from head to foot!; twenty days from today to Easter Monday, and I am cold and tired, without fire and shelter; I shall remember, O Christ, that I am writing to thee, because I am fatigued today.[19]

The fifteenth-century copyist of a manuscript that records the customs of Tallaght disclaims all responsibility for the contents of his text by adding the comment 'Whoever finds it tedious, I have written this book as I found it.'[20] The scribe who copied the *Life* of Ciaran of Clonmacnoise in the *Book of Lismore* also blames the manuscript he copied for the obscurities in his own text, declaring that 'It is not I that am answerable for the meaningless words that are in this Life but the bad [original].'[21]

On other occasions, however, the scribes took time to express their contentment in their work in spite of its trying nature. The following lines are from a poem that is attributed to Colm Cille, but which was probably written in the late eleventh or twelfth century:

> My hand is weary with writing ...;
> A steady stream of wisdom springs from my well coloured neat
>   fair pen ...

I send my little dripping pen unceasingly over an
assemblage of books of great beauty, to enrich the
possessions of the men of art ...[22]

A somewhat similar message is conveyed in a story that occurs in the
Yellow Book of Lecan. The writer makes the point that although the
effort in making poetry is wearisome and trying the finished poem is the
source of lasting satisfaction and pleasure. Poetry is, he declares, like a
cow that never goes dry.[23]

The Irish author of a work that was composed towards the end of
the seventh century expressed the hope that the Lord who preferred the
widow's mite to the abundant gold of the rich, and who received gifts of
gold and silver and precious stones in the Temple in Jerusalem, would
not despise the good will of those who, like the writer, presented their
'goat-skins', that is, the manuscripts they had written, as their offering
to their God.[24]

A VARIETY OF SCHOLARS

The compilers of the Annals frequently refer to different kinds of schol-
ars. The highest position was held by the master of Latin learning and
Scripture, and he enjoyed a status equal to that of a king, a bishop and a
chief poet. He is regularly referred to as sapiens, 'sage', in Hiberno-
Latin and as *suí litre* or *fer léigind*, 'lecturer, master of studies', in Irish.[25]
The Annals record the death of over sixty such scholars. Thus, for
example, we find the following entry for the year 823 in the Annals of
Inisfallen: 'The invasion of Bennchor (Bangor) by the heathens (the
Norse) and the shrine of Comgall (founder of Bangor) was broken by
them, and its learned men and its bishops (a suíd agus a hepscoip) were
put to the sword.'[26]

In the entries for the years between about 900 and 1100 the Annals
mention the deaths of sixteen specialists in law, called *brithem* in Irish
and *iudex* in Latin. It is explicitly stated that some of these held high
ecclesiastical offices, and it is to be presumed that this was the case for
many of the others as well. From a study of the Annals between the
ninth and the twelfth centuries D. O'Corráin has concluded that the
practice of law was very much in the hands of clerics in this period, and
in that context he adds that an examination of earlier legal tracts justifies
the conclusion that churchmen had a great influence on legal development at a much earlier date.[27] An examination of several texts of a legal
nature enabled L. Breatnach to draw the following conclusion:

... for eighth-century Munster we can hardly speak of secular
law-schools uninfluenced by christianity. Rather, the evidence
presented above provides firm support for the integration of the
churches into Irish society as a whole, the involvement of churchmen in the law, and their close family connections with the
secular learned orders ...[28]

The role of ecclesiastics in the development of the legal system is
implicitly acknowledged in the legend, which dates from the early
twelfth century, that St Patrick played a leading part in the drawing up
of the great legal compilation known as the *Senchas Már*. According to
the legend this legal corpus was the work of a commission of three bishops, one of whom was St Patrick, three kings and three *filid* or poets.
One of these 'poets' is described as 'an expert in the native law'. This
team abrogated from the native Irish law everything that was contrary to
Christian principles, and they stipulated that not a single article could be
rescinded by an Irish judge.[29]

Between the eighth and the twelfth centuries the Annals record the
deaths of twenty *seanchaid*, that is, genealogists-cum-historians. Fourteen
of these are explicitly linked with monasteries. These 'historians' frequently compiled or rather created their 'histories' in order to support
the contemporary status quo and to legitimize the claims of their
patrons.[30] During the same period the Annals mention about fifty *filid*,
that is poets and storytellers, and nine of these are said to have been
members of monastic communities. The fact that the Annals do not
explicitly say that the *seanchaidh* or *fili* did not belong to a monastery
does not prove that he had no monastic affiliations. In fact there are
indications that the opposite was often the case.[31]

The following passage from a text on ecclesiastical grades and their
status which dates from about the year 1000 provides evidence that certain learned personalities held official positions in at least the more
important monasteries and that their status depended on the status of
the monastery:

> As for the bishop of Armagh, he has (as his honour-price) twenty
> one *cumals* (female slaves), and furthermore his man of ecclesiasti-
> cal learning (a *fer legind*) and his chief judge and poet have the
> same honour-price as him; and it is thus even for every man of
> ecclesiastical learning and poet and judge of every other
> monastery, that he has the same honour-price as his bishop.[32]

CONFIDENT IN THEIR LEARNING

Whatever may be said about the legal status of scholars in early medieval Ireland they themselves took pride in their profession and were confident in their own tradition. Writing in 613 to Pope Boniface IV St Columbanus justifies his boldness in penning what is a rather outspoken letter to the Supreme Pontiff by saying that 'the freedom of my country's customs, to put it so, has been part cause of my audacity. For amongst us it is not a man's station but his principles that matter.'[33] In a letter written in 593 to Pope Gregory the Great Columbanus indignantly rejected the scheme for establishing the date of Easter which had been drawn up by Victorius of Aquitaine between the years 461 and 468. He wrote:

> For you must know that Victorius has not been accepted by our teachers, by the former scholars of Ireland, by the mathematicians most skilled in reckoning chronology, but has earned ridicule or indulgence rather than authority.[34]

Study and reading formed a regular part of the monk's regime as we gather from the *Lives of the Saints* and from the monastic rules that survive. Adomnán's *Life of Columba*, for example, frequently mentions that Colm Cille or his companions were engaged in study or reading.[35] A seventh century hymn in honour of St Comgall, founder of the monastery of Bangor, says of him that he was 'learned in the Scriptures, ... a distinguished scholar in the canonical writings of the Old Testament and in the Acts of the New'.[36] Among the customs of the monastery of Kileigh (near Tullamore) were 'perseverance in learning, ... listening to the elders, ... searching the scriptures, ... relating the Gospels'.[37] Unlike the Desert Fathers the Irish anchorites favoured study. The *Rule of Colm Cille*, which was probably composed in the ninth century and which was intended for solitaries, enjoins that the monk's day is to be spent in 'prayers, work, and reading'.[38] The importance of study for the person who is striving for sanctity is brought out in the story about the teacher (*magister*) who approached the virgin Samthann of Clonbroney and said, 'I am minded to put aside study and to give myself to prayer.' To whom the saint: 'What shall maintain thy mind against straying thought if thou neglect spiritual studies?'[39]

CONCLUSION

The Irish learned the art of writing only in the fifth century AD. However, they learned quickly, and by the year 600 they were producing texts of quality in both Latin and Irish. By this time too, as we know from the texts that have come down to us, they were becoming familiar with the writings of the Latin Fathers and with the Latin learning of early mediaeval Europe. Their appreciation of books and their eagerness to possess them comes across in a story that has been handed down in several manuscripts. The story tells how three people who were together in a church were asked with what they would like to fill the church in which they stood. When the first two had expressed their wishes, the third man, Cummine the Tall by name, spoke up in the following terms:

> I should like it [the church] full of books, for them to go to the students, and to sow God's word in the ears of everyone, [so as] to bring them to heaven out of the track of the devil.[40]

If the Irish appreciated books and held scholars in esteem there were those who occasionally expressed reservations about the value of learning and scholarship. Such a one was the author of the following quatrains:

> 'Tis sad to see the sons of learning
> In everlasting Hellfire burning
> While he that never read a line
> Doth in eternal glory shine ...
>
> Learning and philosophy are vain,
> Reading, grammar and gloss,
> Diligent literature and metrics,
> Small their avail in heaven above.[41]

The sentiments expressed in these lines run counter to nearly everything we have written in this article, and they might seem to be a poor choice for our final quotation. But we quote them simply because they are unusual in ancient Irish literature, and because they express a point of view that was never accepted by the monks and the learned class of ancient Ireland who always loved books, honoured scribes, and held scholarship in high esteem.

NOTES

1 See K. Hughes, *Early Christian Ireland: Introduction to the Sources* (London, 1972), pp. 53-6.

2 Ogham writing, which was based on the Latin alphabet and which consisted of a series of lines on either side of or intersecting a straight line, had developed in the period from the third to the fifth centuries. It is found mainly in inscriptions on standing stones.

3 In Christian literature the druids often appear as anti-Christian magicians; see, for example, the seventh-century *Life* of Patrick by Muirchú where Patrick and a druid engage in a thaumaturgical contest before King Loeghaire of Tara to determine whether Christianity was superior to druidism or vice versa. The king suggested that both men place their books in water, and he whose books would be recovered in a dry condition would be the victor. Patrick was willing to take up the contest but the druid withdrew; see L. Bieler, *The Patrician Texts in the Book of Armagh* (Dublin, 1979), p. 95.

4 See P.J. Corish, 'The Christian Mission', in P.J. Corish (ed.), *A History of Irish Catholicism*, vol. I/3 (Dublin, 1972), pp. 2-7.

5 See *Life of Colm Cille, compiled by Manus O'Donnell in 1532*, ed. and trans. by A. O'Kelleher and G. Schoepperle (Chicago, 1918; reprint Dublin, 1994), pp. 354-5.

6 See W. Stokes, *The Tripartite Life of Patrick with Other Documents Relating to the Saint*, 2 vols (London, 1887), ii, pp. 403-4.

7 W. Stokes, *Félire Oengusso Céle Dé. The Martyrology of Oengus the Culdee* (London, 1905; reprint Dublin, 1984), pp. 24-6.

8 See K. McCone, *Pagan Past and Christian Present* (Maynooth, 1990), pp. 203-32; and idem, 'Dán agus Tallann', in P. Ó Fiannachta (ed.), *Léann na Cléire* (Léachtaí Cholm Cille XVI) (Maigh Nuad, 1986), pp. 9-53, especially pp. 42-53.

9 Gerald of Wales, *The History and Topography of Ireland*, trans. with an Introduction by J.J. O'Meara (London, 1982), p. 84.

10 We must remember that there are scholars who claim that the Book of Durrow was not produced in Ireland but in Northumbria or in Scotland.

11 See H. Wasserschleben (ed.), *Die irische Kanonensammlung*, 2nd ed. (Leipzig, 1885), p. 1.

12 See W. Stokes, *Félire Oengusso*, op. cit., p. 270. The writer explicitly mentions the works of Ambrose, Hilary, Jerome and Eusebius among the texts he had consulted.

13 See K. Meyer, *Learning in Ireland in the Fifth Century and the Transmission of Letters* (Dublin, 1913), p. 11.

14 See R.I. Best and O. Bergin (eds.), *Lebor na hUidre* (Dublin, 1929), p. 94; trans. D. O'Corráin, 'Nationality and kingship in pre-Norman Ireland', in T.W. Moody (ed.), *Nationality and the Pursuit of National Independence* (Belfast, 1978), p. 19.

15 See K. Ryan, 'Holes and Flaws in Medieval Irish Manuscripts', *Peritia*, 6-7, (1987-88), pp. 243-64, especially pp. 249-50.

16 K. Hughes, 'The Distribution of Irish Scriptoria and Centres of Learning from 730 to 1111', in N.K. Chadwick et al. (eds.), *Studies in the Early British Church* (Cambridge, 1958), pp. 243-72.

17 See W. Stokes and J. Strachan, *Thesaurus Paleo-Hibernicus*, 2 vols. (Cambridge, 1901-3; reprint Dublin, 1975), ii, pp. xix-xxii.

18 See G. Murphy, *Early Irish Lyrics. Eighth to Twelfth Century* (Oxford, 1956), p. 5.

19 E. Hull, *Early Christian Ireland* (London and Dublin, 1905), pp. 224-5. For other marginal glosses in the *Leabhar Breac* see Peter O'Dwyer, 'Irish Medieval Spirituality' in M. Maher (ed.), *Irish Spirituality* (Dublin, 1981), pp. 57-70, especially pp. 67-8.

20 E.J. Gwynn and W.J. Purton, 'The Monastery of Tallaght', *Proceedings of the Royal Irish Academy*, vol. 29 (1911), pp. 115-78, especially p. 119.

21 W. Stokes (ed.), *Lives of Saints from the Book of Lismore* (Oxford, 1890), p. 280.

22 Murphy, *Early Irish Lyrics*, op. cit., pp. 70-1.

23 See R. Flower, *The Irish Tradition* (Oxford, 1947; reprint Dublin, 1994), pp. 70-71.

24 M.C. Díaz y Díaz, *Liber de Ordine Creaturarum. Un Anónimo irlandés del siglo VII* (Santiago de Compostella, 1972), pp. 203-4.

25 It is not easy to decide whether the Annals make a clear distinction between the *fer léigind* and the scribe. The latter term is rarely mentioned after the early tenth century. Kenney believes that the use of *fer léigind* in later texts in place of 'scribe' simply indicates a shifting of emphasis from Latin to Irish; see J.F. Kenney, *The Sources for the Early History of Ireland: Ecclesiastical. An Introduction and Guide* (Columbia: 1929; reprint Shannon, 1968; etc.), p. 11. On the other hand K. Hughes thinks that the evidence indicates that the different terms referred to different functions; K. Hughes, 'The Distribution ...', op. cit., pp. 247-8. Yet she says that the scribe was 'probably also in charge of the monastic school' (ibid., p. 247).

26 S. Mac Airt (ed.), *The Annals of Inisfallen* (Dublin, 1951), p. 125.

27 See O'Corráin, 'Nationality and kingship ...', op. cit., pp. 14-16.

28 L. Breatnach, 'Canon Law and Secular Law in Ireland: The Significance of *Bretha Nemed*', *Peritia* (1984), pp. 439-59; the quotation is from p. 459.

29 See D.A. Binchy, 'The Pseudo-historical Prologue to the *Senchas Már*', *Studia Celtica*, vols 10-11 (1975-6), pp. 15-28.

30 See H. Moisl, 'The Church and the Native Tradition of Learning in Early Medieval Ireland', in P. Ní Chatháin and M. Richter, *Irland und die Christenheit. Ireland and Christendom. Bibel Studien und Mission. The Bible and the Missions* (Stuttgart, 1987), pp. 258-71.

31 See McCone, *Pagan Past . . .*, op. cit., pp. 22-5; idem, Dán Agus Tallann, op. cit., pp. 11-13.

32 See D.A. Binchy (ed.), *Corpus Iuris Hibernici*, 6 vols. (Dublin, 1978), vi, p. 2102; translation from L. Breatnach, *Uraicecht na Ríar. The Poetic Grades in Early Irish Law* (Dublin, 1987), p. 91.

33 See G.S.M. Walker, *Sancti Columbani Opera* (Dublin, 1970), p. 49.

34 Walker, *Sancti Columbani Opera*, op. cit., p. 7.

35 See A.O. Anderson and M.O. Anderson (eds.), *Adomnan's Life of Columba* (Edinburgh, 1961), pp. 207, 257, 279, 299, etc.

36 I. Adamson, *Bangor Light of the World*, 2nd ed. (Belfast, 1987), p. 205.

37 Kuno Meyer, *Texts, Documents and Extracts, chiefly from Manuscripts in the Bodleian and Other Oxford Lirbaries (Anecdota Oxoniensia)* (Oxford, 1894), pp. 41-2.

38 Cf. A.W. Haddan and W. Stubbs, *Councils and Ecclesiastical Documents Relating to Great Britain and Ireland*, 3 vols. (Oxford, 1869-73), ii, pp. 119-21. On the place of the scriptures and scripture studies in the lives of the Irish saints see M. Ó Meachair, *Scrúdú na Scrioptúr* (Dublin, 1994), pp. 64-74.

39 See C. Plummer, *Vitae Sanctorum Hiberniae*, 2 vols. (Oxford, 1910), ii, p. 260; trans. Flower, *The Irish Tradition*, op. cit., p. 58.

40 See W. Stokes, *Lives of Saints*, op. cit, pp. 303-304.

41 See Flower, *The Irish Tradition*, op. cit, p. 46; G. Calder (ed.), *Auraicept na n-Eces. The Scholars' Primer* (Edinburgh, 1917; reprint Dublin, 1995), pp. 6-7.

The Poet and the Word:
Spirituality in the Work of Patrick Kavanagh

UNA AGNEW

THE POET IS ON THE TRACK OF THE GODS

Gaston Bachelard, an admired French philosopher, sees the poet as a dreamer of words. A poet dreams into the interiority of words, sounds out their extremities and explores their infinities.[1] Patrick Kavanagh (1904-67), in his poems, uncovered 'the immortal in things mortal'.[2] He is clear as to his mission: 'the poet is a theologian'.[3] His theological method may be unorthodox, yet, he performs a prophetic role for society by re-membering and re-interpreting God for others in symbols and images amenable to all. He is quick to notice 'God's breath in common statement'[4] and to build, through poetry, a new 'city of God' when the old one has been despoiled by consumerism, hypocrisy and neglect of spiritual values. Alert to the situation, the poet rings out his warning to herald the advent of a counter-cultural revolution.

> But hope, the poet comes to build
> A new city, high above lust and logic,
> The trucks of language overflow, and magic
> At every turn of the living road is spilled.
> *A Wreath for Thomas Moore*

In his essay entitled 'What Are Poets For?', Heidegger asserts that the world is in danger of losing its sacrality. The poet, he believes, is the one who senses 'the trace of the fugitive gods' and stays on their tracks' as if to retrace a path back to the holy.[5] No poet does this better than Kavanagh who raises 'a cut-away bog' 'in a backward place' to the dignity of God's trysting place with the soul. The moment is attended by 'anonymous' but splendidly attired wild-flower performers:

> ... an important occasion as the Muse at her toilet
> Prepares to inform the local farmer
> That beautiful, beautiful, beautiful God
> Was breathing His love by a cut-away God.
> *The One*

42

AWAKENING OF KAVANAGH'S MYSTICAL IMAGINATION

Kavanagh believed that the poet was particularly susceptible to the direct influence of the Holy Ghost. 'The Holy Ghost' he says, 'will not enter the soul that has not within it a secret room, free from vulgarity'.[6] He tells how he tried to communicate his vision of fields, hills and weeds to his neighbours who only encountered his musings with incomprehension and ridicule. In his autobiography, Kavanagh recalls cycling with his brother to a football-match in Dundalk. On the way, he experienced something which, even his brother did not understand:

> 'Do you see anything very beautiful and strange on those hills?'
> 'This free-wheel is missing' he said and he gave it a vigorous
>   crack with the heel of his shoe. 'Is it on Dromgonnelly hills?'
> 'Yes.'
> 'Do you mean the general beauty of the landscape?'
> 'Something beyond that, beyond that'. I said
> 'Them hills are fine no doubt'.
> 'And is that all you see?'
> 'This free-wheel is missing again,' he said'I'll have to get down
>   and put a drop of oil on it'.
> We go moving again. 'What were we talking about?'
> 'Beauty,' I said. [*GF*, p. 201]

This short passage signals the awakening of the emerging poet's consciousness. Mystical imagination is juxtaposed with the prosaic necessity expressed in his brother's statement – 'this free-wheel is missing again' – or the even more vision-dampening question: 'Do you mean the general beauty of the landscape?' Kavanagh was gradually becoming aware of the lonely world of the poet who is little understood, even by his own brother. Writing for a Dublin girl (Joan Russell), whom he loved, Kavanagh asked

> indulgence for his eccentric ways:
> And pray ...
> For him who walked apart
> On the hills
> Loving life's miracles ...
>   *Joan Russell*

When Kavanagh mentioned his vision of light on the hills, he knew he was speaking of 'a beauty beyond beauty'. His experience is reminiscent of the 'I-know-not-what' experienced by the Spanish mystic, St John of the Cross when he searches for words to describe divine things which are unnameable;[7] 'things which eye hath not seen nor ear heard' (1 Cor 2:9). Many of Kavanagh's neighbours, seeing him on occasion rapt in wonder at the landscape, thought he was 'gettin' a bit odd of himself' (*GF*, p. 200). Soon he learned to conceal his vision and match his neighbours in 'vulgar talk' until he admits; 'I was the most vulgar man in the company' (*GF*, p. 187).

Vulgarity, however, 'went against the grain of his soul,' but it *did* become a second nature, hiding his poetic soul, except to trusted friends. His wife, Katherine Moloney, admired him greatly; 'There goes all I know of God' was her favourite description of her husband who had been her friend of long-standing. For the majority of people, the nobler aspects of the poet's personality were hidden under a rough exterior. The word, became virtually the sole vehicle of communicating his inner dialogue with God and self.

KAVANAGH'S LITURGY OF THE EARTH

Kavanagh's early work reflects a naive and primitive turn of mind. He belonged to the earth and the soil. In his early poem *To the Man after the Harrow*, he intuitively grasps, through the metaphors of harrowing and sowing, the power inherent in clay. The farmer was participating in God's work. The poet's ability to penetrate earthy symbols leads him to uncover suffering as part of the human condition. Symbols of working the soil insert the poet firmly into biblical territory: 'Unless the grain of wheat fall to the ground and die it remains only a single grain' (John 12:24). Seed and poet travel the same precarious inner route; both undergo purification as they journey towards a hidden destiny. The poem moves steadily forward, in rhythmic quatrains, secure in its dual purpose and resounding with its message of hope: 'For you/ Are driving your horses through/ The mist where Genesis begins.' A spiritual enterprise of mythical proportions has begun, and all of it rooted in clay!

Whether ploughing, harrowing, sowing or pulling weeds, Kavanagh had easy access to the sacred dimension of the earth. The philosopher Eliade, points out that this affinity with the hierophanic nature of earth and labour is a quality which still survives among the rural population of contemporary Europe. 'The cosmos being a hierophany, and human existence sacred, work possessed a liturgical value ...'[8] Kavanagh's poetry undoubtedly testifies to the truth that simplest farm task was thoroughly immersed in the divine and imbued with liturgical significance. Not only had he the ability to 'find a star-lovely art/ in a dark sod' but instinctively followed the changes of the seasons as an ever-unfolding liturgy. He continues to bring to light, new and original manifestations of God as he perceived them in his native landscape. The first bright yellow coltsfoot, he humorously suggests, is a model of christian faith, bravely making its 'gap in winter's wall' and overcoming the dead earth. Faith in life is Kavanagh's self professed creed:

> O give me faith
> That I may be
> Alive when April's
> Ecstasy
> Dances in every
> White-thorn tree.   *A Prayer for Faith*

There is a hint of pagan worship in Kavanagh's early white-thorn dance. He attributed his early access to the sacred as privilege afforded him by 'the gods of poetry ... who 'give every young poet...one peep into every tabernacle ... (*GF*, pp. 200-1). He broke away eventually from these pagan leanings as well as from the poetic diction of the school-books and found his authentic voice in the speech rhythms, and religious thought-patterns of his native parish. The poem *April* catches Kavanagh in the act of turning away from some dimly-lit pagan temple and entering the great christian celtic church of the out-of-doors. In quiet unadorned tones, he enters imaginatively into the liturgy of the Incarnation, Inniskeen-style! The 'green meadows' where the Virgin Mary conceives are the fields of Mucker and Shancoduff!

> Now is the hour we rake out the ashes
> Of the spirit-fires winter-kindled.
> (This is surely the language of Victorian school-books.)[9]
> We dare not leave it
> Dark, unlovely, deserted.
> Level! O level it down!
> Here we are building a bright new town.
>
> The old cranky spinster is dead
> Who fed us cold flesh
> And in the green meadows

> The maiden of Spring is with child
> By the Holy Ghost.
>
> *April*

By 1947, when his novel *Tarry Flynn* has been completed, we hear an unmistakeable Christian cry of exultation over a field of turnips:

> The Holy Ghost was taking the Bedlam of little fields and making it into a song, a simple song which he could understand. And he saw the Holy Spirit on the hills.[10]

Moved by the ecstasy of the moment Tarry 'loosed the horse ... and let the mare out on the grass,' as if all creation, human and brute-beast alike, must participate in the new life of spring – a life emanating from the energy of the Holy Spirit.

KAVANAGH FINDS HIS VOICE AS A CHRISTIAN POET

The early sonnet *Primrose*, is evidence of a poetic voice that has become more confident in its vision and diction:

> Upon a bank I sat, a child made seer
> Of one small primrose flowering in my mind.
> Better than wealth it is, said I, to find
> One small page of Truth's manuscript made clear.
> I looked at Christ transfigured without fear—
> The light was very beautiful and kind,
> And where the Holy Ghost in flame had signed
> I read it through the lenses of a tear ...
>
> *Primrose*

The recurring reference to the Holy Ghost is noteworthy in Kavanagh's work, a presence signed in flame at the heart of the primrose. The imagery is neither forced nor fictionalized. Kavanagh has learned that the beauty of truth surpasses fabrication or fantasy. Neither does he engage in mere pantheistic rationalization. Kavanagh was always well aware that the reality of God or Christ lay *beyond* the image, symbol and metaphor, however alluring these might be.

The primrose revelation of Christ is brought a step further and raised to the level of epiphany at the end of Kavanagh's poem *Advent*.

Epiphanies in Kavanagh were momentary revelations – moments of brightening vision. The movement in *Advent* towards illumination is gradual, yet inevitable. The soul, seeking to restore its lost sense of wonder, undergoes voluntary disciplines familiar to the mystic: purification, darkness and re-awakening. Ritual seasonal cleansing restores the poet's sense of wonder – 'the wonder of a child's soul'. *Advent* points to a new belief in 'the everydays of life,' the 'ordinary plenty' of people who live simply and frugally. This enriched vision reaches its climax in the unexpected radiance of an early spring bloom, escaping the cold imprisoned earth ... Kavanagh is contemplatively alert to its spiritual significance as he states simply: 'And Christ comes with a January flower.'

Kavanagh's finest epiphany is executed, once again in sonnet form (a thirteen-line sonnet!) for the downcast inhabitants of *The Great Hunger*. For Paddy Maguire, the prototype of many Irish small farmers in the 1930s and 40s, there is little joy. He lives a defeated existence, the awfulness of which is figuratively depicted as being 'locked in a stable with pigs and cows forever'. Nevertheless, for one or two rare moments, the inhabitants of *The Great Hunger*, are pervious to inklings of transcendence.

Kavanagh, a film-critic for the *Standard*, shows aptitude as cameraman poet. He moves in for a close-up of Maguire at work. A new season is making its cold entrance in the dim atmosphere of South Monaghan. Maguire has set his teeth to the task of once more ploughing his few fields, attended by the dreaded black, east wind 'blowing from Dundalk'. He has little support from his neighbours who resent his progress, watching enviously 'from every second hill'. Revelation is as unexpected as the casual posture of Maguire suggests, whose greatest annoyance is that he 'forgot to bring his matches'. Yet, suddenly, a transcendent beauty awakens the landscape as a wintry shaft of sunlight shines through 'Brannigan's gap'. At once the terrain is bathed in a radiant warmth. A new and unexpected energy floods the land, bringing traces of hope, revelation and transcendent beauty:

> The pull is on the traces it is March
> And a cold black wind is blowing from Dundalk.
> The twisting sod rolls over on her back
> The virgin screams before the irresistible sock.
> No worry on Maguire's mind this day
> Except that he forgot to bring his matches.
> From every second hill a neighbour watches

With all the sharpened interest of rivalry.
Yet sometimes when the sun comes through a gap
These men see God the Father in a tree:
The Holy Spirit is the rising sap,
And Christ will be the green leaves that will come
At Easter from the sealed and guarded tomb.

The Great Hunger, stanza III

The faith-life of a rural townland is mystically illumined by a ray of sunshine. The poet knew well the quality of rural faith and its affinity for living symbols of God. He knew neighbours, who loved the ageless permanence of trees, who reverenced lone bushes that stood intact despite the cold of winter and dearth of fuel. He knew also the perennial excitement occasioned by the rising sap, the spiritual anticipation of Easter and the hope engendered by a new season. Here, in this excerpt of *The Great Hunger*, Kavanagh has discovered his own symbolic rendering of the Trinity, the central doctrine of his faith. This is a dynamic theology – a Unity and Trinity enfolding a rural community, inserted into the fabric of their daily lives and historical roots, filled with transcendent beauty.

GOD PRESENT IN THE LOCAL: THE INCARNATE GOD

For Kavanagh, God's rightful place was situated squarely among His people. He decried the advent of 'continental Catholicism' promoted in Ireland after the Synod of Thurles in 1850, which ousted the oldfashioned piety associated with stations, holy wells, pilgrimages, saints days and cross-road dancing ... and removed a home-based religion to the post-Emancipation chapel, at a distance from peoples' lives. Places of worship, which before were Mass-rocks, old barns and kitchens, were now large cold buildings, located, preferably, on top of a hill. One had to dress appropriately to go there. The post-Synod-of-Thurles priest was directed to adopt 'black or dark' attire and was recommended to keep his distance from local patterns, pilgrimages to holy wells, faction fights and merry-making.[11] Instead, there emerged a rash of continental devotions, Missions, Novenas and Confraternities which changed the face of Irish Catholicism.[12] Kavanagh, tongue in cheek, describes his little room over the kitchen where he slept and wrote:

10 by 12
And a low roof
If I stand by the side wall
My head feels the reproof.

Five holy pictures
Hang on the walls
The Virgin and Child
St Anthony of Padua
Leo the XIII
St Patrick and the Little Flower.

My bed in the centre
So many things to me –
A writing table
And a slumber palace.

My room in a dusty attic
But its little window
Lets in the stars.
My Room

This early poem introduces us to the poet as comic writer and critic. Imported repository religion, Kavanagh warned, could cramp the inner aspirations of the soul. God, he knew, was beyond the grasp of numerical religion. The 'nine Fridays devotion' drew from him some of his more caustic remarks. He roundly exposes those parishioners, well known for backbiting gossip, who boasted undying support for the devotion. The anti-hero Tarry Flynn, voices the criticism, all the more effective because it is laced with humour:

> On the first Friday of every month..(they) could be seen strolling home from the village church, their sharp tongues in keeping with their sharp noses. Tarry, when he reflected on this devotion, was glad that he had gone through it, for there was a story that anyone who had done so would never die unrepentant. That gave a man a great chance to have a good time. [*TF*, p. 28]

Paddy Maguire of *The Great Hunger* is similarly trapped in an outer observance that is bereft of inner disposition:

> 'Now go to Mass and pray and confess your sins
> And you'll have all the luck,' his mother said.
>
> *The Great Hunger*, stanza VII

The tragedy for Paddy Maguire was that he 'listened to lie' and 'took it as literal truth.' He sadly lacked the poet's ability to transcend cliché and discover his own 'star'.

THE ART OF OUTRAGEOUS JUXTAPOSITION

As a further ploy to reinstate God in the local, Kavanagh employs the technique of 'unlikely juxtaposition' as if to make a plea for some degree of integrated spirituality. One of the poet's most successful instances of this occurs in *The Long Garden*. He looks with longing at his idyllic childhood place, home of opposites. Yet this is the birthplace of his faith and his imagination:

> It was the garden of the golden apples
> A long garden between a railway and a road
> In the sow's rooting where the hen scratches
> We dipped our fingers in the pockets of God.[12]
>
> *The Long Garden*

No more unlikely place to discover God's bountiful presence than in the 'sow's rooting' or 'where the hen scratches! Further spiritual surprises are to be found 'among decent men, who barrow dung in gardens under trees' (*Advent*). To redress the balance in favour of the created universe which, was is in danger of being slighted by current theological argument, Kavanagh places Bethlehem at the heart of his own parish, finds his own local star 'over Cassidy's hanging hill', and sees 'three (local) whin bushes' take on the role of Magi in disguise.[13] This local orchestral rendering of God-come-among-us, reaches a crescendo in Kavanagh's late harvest of poems 1955-8, when God arrives 'down in the marshes' in a colourful riot of 'Green, blue, yellow and red ...' (*The One*).

By using his juxtaposition technique, Kavanagh was unconsciously following an age-old celtic tradition. The scribes and illuminators of ancient manuscripts often drew cats, mice, otters and angels in their illuminations of letters in the biblical text, at moments of holiest import.[14] In his poetic work Kavanagh took delight in moving the things of heaven and the things of earth into closer proximity. 'Bits of roads' become 'eternal lanes of joy' while 'particular trees' serve to hold him in 'their mysteries.[15]

A SACRAMENTAL IMAGINATION

The crown of Kavanagh's poetic gift must surely be his sacramental imagination. At moments of intense lyricism he saw 'the immortal in things mortal' which he radiantly captured in such phrases as: 'moonlight that lives forever in a tree' and in 'fields that were part of no earthly estate'.[16] He continues to exercise his sacramental imagination until he discovers, that everything speaks of God; 'Nothing whatever is by love debarred'.[17] He thrills at the 'inexhaustible adventure of a gravelled yard' which another might treat as commonplace. Recovered from illness and sense of failure in 1955, his humbled ego learns gratitude, serenity and a new lyrical energy. A colourful and invigorated God 'is down in the bogs and marshes' of his native landscape while the same God walks 'the unconscious streets of Dublin'. In the tradition of the great Julian of Norwich, who acknowledges God's motherhood, Kavanagh unselfconsciously celebrates God as woman:

> Surely my God is feminine, for Heaven
> Is the generous impulse, is contented
> With feeding praise to the good. And all
> Of these that I have known have come from women.
> While men the poet's tragic light resented
> The spirit that is Woman caressed his soul.
>
> *God in Woman*

Along the Grand Canal, near Leeson Street Bridge, his 'leafy-with-love banks' ... are sacramentally alive; they 'are pouring redemption' for him. Interiorly he has been transformed. His soul, reborn, now needs to be honoured with a new baptismal dress. He has outgrown his ideal of childhood prayer 'like a white rose pinned/ On the Virgin Mary's blouse,'[18] and calls for an attire, a vestment, appropriate to the moment:

> For this soul need to be honoured with a new dress woven
> From green and blue things and arguments that cannot be proven.
>
> *Canal Bank Walk*

The poet exults in God's will which has ordained that he be, what he always was, a poet of the ordinary. His poetic voice, Augustine Martin notices, has become poised and assured.[19] He is aware of the miracle of healing which has accompanied his narrow escape from lung cancer and despair. He glows in the new harvest of poems which testify to a renewed vision, born of inner transformation and repose.

KAVANAGH IMAGES GOD

Throughout his writings Kavanagh ponders the notion of God under many guises. God, it can be said, was one of his 'pet' subjects. He wrote of the mechanized God of the catechism and of novenas, the blood-and-thunder God of the Redemptorist Mission, the cruel-to-be-kind God of *Lough Derg* who delights 'in disillusionment' and the elusive God ardently sought in His totality, figuratively depicted as 'the Absolute envased bouquet'. In more abstract vein, but well within the walls of orthodoxy, Kavanagh in hushed tone mentions the ineffable God:

> ... the door whose combination lock has puzzled
> Philosopher and priest and common dunce.
> *The Great Hunger*, stanza VI

During his early life as a poet, Kavanagh wrote with confidence of the God he had imbibed in Church, school and family. Emerging from personal failure, humiliation and defeat in the 1950s, Kavanagh clung to a new depth of belief learning something new about the true nature of God:

> I learned, I learned – when one might be inclined
> To think, too late, you cannot recover your losses –
> I learned something of the nature of God's mind
> Not the abstract Creator but He who caresses
> The daily and nightly earth; He who refuses
> To take failure for an answer till again and again is worn.
> *Miss Universe*

In more humorous vein, Kavanagh imaginatively encounters God and the Devil in two separate, but related poems.[20] With the deliberate juxtaposition of these two pieces, Kavanagh explodes assumptions that God's attributes are those of middle-class respectability. At first sight, Kavanagh seems almost blasphemous in addressing topics generally reserved for priests and theologians. There were many in the Dublin of his time who would have denounced him as irreligious. Yet, Kavanagh succeeds through his humour, in exploding false myths, in exploring the otherness of God and in challenging accepted religious values.

In teasing out the meaning of a God who 'must be allowed to surprise us,' he unconsciously assumes the role of spiritual guru:

We must be nothing, nothing
that God may make us something.

Having Confessed

Ultimately, Kavanagh's God 'caresses, the daily and nightly earth' and
the earth returns the compliment:

The raving flowers looked up in the face
Of the One and the Endless, the Mind that has baulked (sic)
The profoundest of mortals.

The One

Immanence and transcendence are exquisitely held in balance by a poet,
who better than almost any other Catholic poet of this century, com-
bines unerring doctrine with intuitive sacramental vision and lyrical
technique to address the tantalizing and often vexed question of God.

KAVANAGH TELLS US WHO WE ARE

One of the most important functions of a poet such as Kavanagh, is that
he tells us, the reader, who we are and where we have come from. Until
recently, Ireland was a predominantly rural culture, Kavanagh portrays
life on the land in the 1930s and 40s in a way no other writer has done.
He captures the 'wink and elbow' language of country people and their
sophisticated methods of sizing up a situation. His cameos of Irish life
are unquestionably authentic: 'someone shouldering home a saddle-
harrow,' 'an old plough upside down on a weedy ridge' 'dandelions
growing on headlands showing their unloved hearts to everyone'. He
describes a way of life that, though passing, was once ours and shaped
our consciousness. He is faithful to the grandeur as well as to the desperation in people's lives.

Kavanagh does not shirk his task of dealing with despair. His *Great
Hunger* is a classic for all who fail to find transcendence in the dreari-
ness of human existence. Kavanagh grasped the nettle of poverty, the
treadmill of small farm life, poor land and unwanted marriagelessness
stemming from over-divided farm holdings as well as repressive
Catholicism of his times. The resulting spectre of 'unlived life' is
grasped by the poet to exorcise its damning power over himself but also
to awaken others to its pernicious influence:

> Life dried in the veins of these women and men
> The grey and grief and unlove,
> The bone in the backs of their hands,
> And the chapel pressing its low ceiling over them.
> > *The Great Hunger*, stanza IX

He reminds us that the 'continental Catholicism' which we imbibed with our mother's milk, was foreign food. This 'Irish' catholicism has been transported to the four corners of the globe. If we had remained closer to our Celtic roots, our missions to indigenous peoples might have been more sympathetic towards native religious mores. And yet, like Kavanagh we can, 'let in the stars'. There is scarcely one among us who does not nod in self-recognition at Kavanagh's perception of God's presence in the little things of nature:

> And when the new moon by her little finger hung
> From the telegraph wires (we) knew how God had happened
> And what the blackbird in the whitethorn sang.
> > *The Long Garden.*[21]

Kavanagh's dedication to the grandeur and dignity of rural life is found in his affirmation of the local:

> I have lived in important places, times
> When great events were decided ...
> > *Epic*

The poet's statement has become the statement of each one. The inhabitant of the smallest, most insignificant townland in Ireland can proclaim with pride. 'I have lived in important places.' Thus the poet cures our far-away-hills-are-greener fantasy and forces us to contemplate things nearby; 'the undying difference in the corner of a field' or 'an old stone lying sideways in a ditch'. These are the 'pearl necklace(s) round the neck of poverty' which Kavanagh unerringly discovers.[22]

CONCLUSION

The word, we have seen, at the hands of the poet can be a powerful instrument; it 'can be a dawn and even a sure shelter'.[23] Whether Kavanagh as a poet is successful in providing a 'dawn' or even a rude 'shelter' for his audience, we must acknowledge that he undertook poetry as his sacred task, 'dabbled in it' until it became his life.[24] He wrote of what he knew best: small-farm rural life, the hedges and ditches of South Monaghan and the importance of God in the lives of rural people. His was not a long-faced spirituality but one that wanted to dance among his native whitethorn hedges. He confronted poverty, spiritual as well as material, and transcended the spectre of 'the great hunger'. Kavanagh's was a spirituality of the ordinary; nothing excluded. His humour led him to make outrageous statements, bringing together moments from the humblest farmyard to commune with mystical delicacies proffered from 'the pockets of God'. He survived the onslaught of his mother's and the Church's pieties by allowing his 'little window' let in 'the stars'. He narrowly escaped despair by looking out 'chance windows of poetry and prayer'.

Happiness, in the end, was his ability 'to snatch out of time the passionate transitory'. 'For we must record love's mystery without claptrap' (*The Hospital*). It is fitting that these are the lines inscribed on his tombstone in Inniskeen. He believed that poetry was an affair of the heart, and an affair of Divine inspiration. He had gifted moments when he saw 'a beauty beyond beauty', and knew a knowledge beyond knowledge. However dishevelled and cantankerous he outwardly appeared, his inner gifts were the fruits of a mystical imagination that cannot be learned in theologates or universities. The poet is eloquent in the manner in which he states this for himself.

> And I have a feeling
> That through a hole in reason's ceiling
> We can fly to knowledge
> Without ever going to college.
>
> *To Hell with Commonsense*

NOTES

1 Gaston Bachelard, *The Poetics of Reverie* (Boston, 1971), pp. 29-54.
2 Patrick Kavanagh, *The Complete Poems*, ed. Peter Kavanagh (New York and Newbridge, 1984), p. 238. Unless otherwise stated all quotations are from this edition which will be referred to by the poem's title or as *CP* with page number.
3 Patrick Kavanagh, *Self Portrait* (Dublin, 1964), p. 28.
4 *Advent CP*, pp. 124-5.

5 Martin Heidegger, 'What are poets for?', *Poetry Language, Thought* (New York, 1971), p. 71.

6 Patrick Kavanagh, *The Green Fool* (London, 1975 ed.), p. 202. All future quotations are from this edition and are referred to as *GF* with page number.

7 St John of the Cross, 'Commentary Applied to Spiritual Things', *The Collected Works of St John of the Cross*, tr. Kieran Kavanagh OCD and Otilio Rodriguez OCD (Washington DC, 1973), pp. 735-7.

8 Mircea Eliade, *The Forge and the Crucible*, trans. Stephen Corrin (New York, 1962), pp. 142-4.

9 'Schoolbook Poetry', *Kavanagh's Weekly*, 10 May 1952.

10 Patrick Kavanagh, *Tarry Flynn* (London, 1978), p. 29. All future quotations are from this edition and are referred to as *TF* with page number.

11 Patrick Corish, *The Irish Catholic Experience: A Historical Survey* (Dublin, 1985), pp. 197-201.

12 Donal Kerr, 'The Early Nineteenth Century, Michael Maher (ed.) *Irish Spirituality* (Dublin, 1981), pp. 135-44.

13 This edition of the poem, which I deem to be the correct one, is found only in *Collected Poems* (London, 1964), p. 74.

14 References to 'Christmas Childhood', *CP*, p. 143.

15 A theme developed by Dr Jennifer O'Reilly of UCC in a paper entitled 'The Book of Kells: The Monastic Reading of Scripture', given at a conference on Celtic spirituality, All Hallows, Dublin, July 1992.

16 *CP*, pp. 274-5.

17 Excerpts from *On Looking into E.V. Rieu's Homer, CP*, p. 238, and *Tarry Flynn, CP*, pp. 141-2 respectively.

18 *The Hospital*, pp. 279-80.

19 *A Christmas Childhood, CP*, pp. 143-5.

20 Augustine Martin, ' "The Apocalypse of Clay": Technique and Vision in "The Great Hunger" ', in Peter Kavanagh (ed.), *Patrick Kavanagh, Man and Poet* (Newbridge, 1987), pp. 286-93.

21 *A View of God and the Devil* and *The Devil, CP*, pp. 208-9.

22 See footnote 13 above.

23 Quotations from *Why Sorrow?* and *The Great Hunger*, stanza VI respectively.

24 Edmond Vandercammen, quoted by Bachelard, footnote 33, p. 47.

25 *Self-Portrait*, p. 19.

The Spiritual Strain in Contemporary Women's Writings: The Witness of Women

MARGARET KELLEHER

> Make us human
> in cadences of change and mortal pain
> and words we can grow old and die in.
> > Eavan Boland, 'Time and Violence'[1]

The title of this paper, 'the spiritual strain in contemporary women's writing', has a deliberate ambivalence. As any dictionary reveals, the word 'strain' possesses various meanings: the first cited by *The Oxford English Dictionary* being 'gain, acquisition; treasure' and hence 'begetting, generation', 'pedigree, lineage, ancestry, descent'; secondly, 'constraint' or 'compulsion', 'an extreme or excessive effort; a straining *at* or *after* some object of attainment'; and, thirdly, 'a musical sequence of sounds; a melody, tune' and thus 'a passage of song or poetry'. All three of these senses are of relevance to a discussion of women's writing, its poetic form, the thematics of constraint and generation. In particular, contemporary women's writing attests to the significance of 'generations', the witness of other women, those who have gone into the future before us.

Within the past twenty years or so, many disciplines or areas of study have experienced the discovery and recovery of women's voices, histories and experiences. In literature, these voices have been found in 'unusual' places, in diaries, letters, folklore and myth, as well as the more typical genres of novel, play and poem. Alice Walker, the African-American novelist, records in her essays the importance of discovering literary works by other black women:

> My discovery of them – most of them out of print, abandoned, discredited, maligned, nearly lost – came about, as many things of value do, almost by accident. As it turned out – and this should not have surprised me – I found I was in need of something that only one of them could provide.[2]

The disappointment and anger of many women readers which greeted

57

the *Field Day Anthology of Irish Writing* arose, at least partly, from those volumes' failure to look for women's voices both in unusual and usual places; while the forthcoming fourth volume promises to restore a large number of women writers to the public domain.

These projects of recovery highlight the creative aspirations and spiritual frustrations of our literary ancestors; in Walker's words,

> these grandmothers and mothers of ours were not Saints, but Artists; driven to a numb and bleeding madness by the springs of creativity in them for which there was no release. They were Creators, who lived lives of spiritual waste, because they were so rich in spirituality – which is the basis of Art – that the strain of enduring their unused and unwanted talent drove them insane.[3]

For their descendants, the absence of literary models constitutes both an obstacle to writing and the motivation to write; recounting Toni Morrison's explanation for writing her novels – 'Because they are the kind of books I want to read' – Walker adds, 'I write all the things *I should have been able to read.*'[4]

Acknowledging the extent to which women have been silent or absent in the tradition has, in turn, generated questions which echo across many disciplines. Why has there been such a silence regarding women's writing and women's experience? How is the tradition changed by the recovery of women's voices – will it be revised, even re-visioned by the speaking of things previously unspoken? Or is the past ever fully recoverable; does an 'unspeakable' remain?

The response by feminist literary critics to these questions falls broadly into two identified schools. The first, often characterised as the 'Anglo-American' school, emphasises the recovery of women's culture, writings and experience and attributes their omission to historical and social factors such as women's limited access to education and publication.[5] French feminist criticism, on the other hand, locates the obstacles to women's expression at the level of language itself, arguing that the 'very construction [of language] is based on presuppositions about gender that devalue women: the speaking or writing subject is constitutively masculine while the silent object is feminine'.[6] According to this view of language, a fundamental contradiction exists between writing and being a woman: 'women's experiences are unrepresentable and women cannot perform acts of representation'.[7]

A further, even more pessimistic, theory of women's relationship to language suggests that the very origins of writing lie in the absence of the female, specifically the mother. As Margaret Homans argues in *Bearing the Word*, her study of language and female experience in the nineteenth century, the founding texts of our culture reveal that 'the death or absence of the mother sorrowfully but fortunately makes possible the construction of language and of culture'.[8] The most recent version of this myth occurs in the account of child development and language by the French psychoanalyst Jacques Lacan in which the son's separation from the mother, his breaking of a preverbal and preoedipal relation, is rewarded by entry into the symbolic order – the 'Law of the father' – the world of language and culture.[9] The mother's absence thus makes language necessary and possible.

*

The poetry of Eavan Boland gives form to both of these theoretical schools; on the one hand, Boland shares in the project of recovering women's experience, seeking, in her own words, to 'bless the ordinary' and 'sanctify the common'[10] – with memorable results. Yet the struggle to find language adequate to that experience also shadows much of her writing. In her long poem, 'The Journey', published in 1986, Boland revises and extends Book VI of Virgil's *Aeneid*, the story of Aeneas' visit to the underworld. The epigraph to the poem relates what happens when Aeneas, wishing to see his father face-to-face, crosses the river of Styx:

> Immediately cries were heard. These were the loud wailing of infant souls weeping at the very entrance-way; never had they had their share of life's sweetness for the dark day had stolen them from their mother's breasts and plunged them to a death before their time.[11]

The woman-narrator of Boland's poem journeys to the underworld, guided by Sappho, the Greek lyric poetess, famous for her poems celebrating women's love. The objects of her journey are the women and children, neglected by history, who have died of pestilence and plague.

> Then to my horror I could see to each
> nipple some had clipped a limpet shape –
> suckling darknesses – while others had their arms
> weighed down, making terrible pietàs.

As one critic has noted, Sappho's arrival is a type of annunciation

scene.[12] Through her guidance, narrator and reader come to recognise
their kinship with those who have died:

> But these are women who went out like you
> when dusk became a dark sweet with leaves,
> recovering the day, stooping, picking up
> teddy bears and rag dolls and tricycles and buckets –
>
> love's archaeology –

And yet the relationship between word and event is not an easy one;
Boland's poem confronts the difficulties of representation, the fear that
what has been seen is 'beyond speech/ beyond song, only not beyond
love'. The narrator seeks to 'at least be their witness' and as poet she, to
some extent, succeeds; yet one of the most powerful legacies of the
poem is the reminder of what lay before 'the word':

> the silences in which are our beginnings,
> in which we have an origin like water.

The challenge of reconstructing what is lost, 'the histories I never
learned/ to predict the lyric of', features in many of Boland's poems.
'Fever', in tones both of regret and great vigour, portrays 'what we lost'
as a 'contagion'

> that breaks out in what cannot be
> shaken out from words or beaten out
> from meaning and survives to weaken
>
> what is given, what is certain
> and burns away everything but this
> exact moment of delirium when
> someone cries out someone's name.[13]

The more recent poem, 'Anna Liffey', suggests Boland's deepening
despair of finding a 'language' for 'the body of an ageing woman':

> And in my late forties
> Past believing
> Love will heal
> What language fails to know
> And needs to say –
> What the body means –[14]

If 'myth is the wound we leave/ in the time we have',[15] Boland's poetry traces the origin and legacy of such wounds, most powerfully in her retellings of the Demeter and Korê myth. The figure of Ceres, the Roman equivalent of Demeter, haunts many of her poems: the goddess who 'rose'

> out of seed, out of wheat,
> out of thawed water
> and went, distracted and astray
> to find her daughter.[16]

The story of Demeter/Ceres, goddess of agriculture, and her daughter, Korê or Persephone, is that of 'the loss of the daughter to the mother, the mother to the daughter'.[17] Performed by the ancient Greeks in the sacred dramas of the Eleusian Mysteries every fall and spring, this myth tells of the abduction and rape of Persephone, daughter of Demeter, by Hades, god of the underworld.[18] Inconsolable, Demeter seeks her daughter all over the world and the earth grows barren as a result of her neglect. The threat of starvation can only be removed if Persephone is returned; yet Hades succeeds in retaining his queen for one third of the year through tricking Persephone into eating addictive pomegranate seeds before she is reunited with her mother. Thus Persephone must return to the underworld for part of the year; while Demeter consents to return fruitfulness to the land for those months in which her daughter is restored to her. This myth clearly functions as an allegory of nature and of seasonal change: Demeter's love for her daughter sets in motion the passage of the seasons; each year her daughter and hence new life return from the dead.

The Demeter/Persephone story is one of loss and reunion, celebrating the renewal of the world, the integration of death and birth, a myth which Adrienne Rich has termed the 'essential female tragedy'.[19] As Rich's study of the experience and institution of motherhood, *Of Woman Born*, explains,

> the role played by the Mysteries of Eleusis in ancient spirituality has been compared to that of the passion and resurrection of Christ. But in the resurrection celebrated by the Mysteries, it is a mother whose wrath catalyzes the miracle, a daughter who rises from the underworld.[20]

This myth has an enduring, evocative power, as Rich's conclusion itself
testifies:

> Each daughter, even in the millennia before Christ, must have
> longed for a mother whose love for her and whose power were so
> great as to undo rape and bring her back from death. And every
> mother must have longed for the power of Demeter, the efficacy
> of her anger, the reconciliation with her lost self.[21]

Eavan Boland's 'The Pomegranate' provides a contemporary retelling:

> The only legend I have ever loved is
> the story of a daughter lost in hell.
> And found and rescued there.
> Love and blackmail are the gist of it.
> Ceres and Persephone the names.[22]

Seeing her 'child asleep beside her teen magazines,/ her can of Coke,
her plate of uncut fruit', the mother can warn her, or, in a poignant and
familiar dilemma, allow her to find her place in the story:

> If I defer the grief I will diminish the gift.
> The legend will be hers as well as mine.
> She will enter it. As I have.
> She will wake up. She will hold
> the papery flushed skin in her hand.
> And to her lips. I will say nothing.

*

The theme of mother and daughter relationships is prevalent in contemporary women's literature, as it is in many other areas of women's writing. If some of the earlier stages of feminism sought to analyse or
rationalise the mother, circumventing or rejecting her role, more recently
women have come to acknowledge and explore the significance of that
relationship, its creative and destructive powers, its intellectual and emotional dimensions. Welcoming this acknowledgement of the 'need' for
our mothers, Rich emphasises, 'The cry of that female child in us need
not be shameful or regressive; it is the germ of our desire to create a
world in which strong mothers and strong daughters will be a matter of
course.'[23] As early as 1929, Virginia Woolf noted that a woman writing
thinks back through her mothers;[24] the titles of some recent women's

writing testify, very lyrically, to this creative source, for example Mary Dorcey's 1991 collection of poems, *Moving into the Space Cleared by Our Mothers*, or Alice Walker's essays, *In Search of Our Mothers' Gardens*.

Walker reminds us that the 'springs of creativity' lay unused in our ancestors' lives: 'Therefore we must fearlessly pull out of ourselves and look at and identify with our lives the living creativity some of our great-grandmothers were not allowed to know.'[25] In a significant qualification, which cautions against equating historical *silence* with *absence*, she continues:

> I stress *some* of them because it is well known that the majority of our great-grandmothers knew, even without 'knowing' it, the reality of their spirituality, even if they didn't recognize it beyond what happened in the singing at church – and they never had any intention of giving it up.[26]

The location of her mother's 'living creativity' is revealed finally, the end of the 'search' movingly simple:

> I notice that it is only when my mother is working in her flowers that she is radiant, almost to the point of being invisible – except as Creator: hand and eye. She is involved in work her soul must have. Ordering the universe in the image of her personal conception of Beauty.

And hence for her daughter, 'Guided by my heritage of a love of beauty and a respect for strength – in search of my mother's garden, I found my own.'[27]

The theme of our relationship to female ancestors, that which is passed on, receives a particularly lyrical expression in Paula Meehan's poem, 'The Pattern':

> Little has come down to me of hers,
> a sewing machine, a wedding band,
> a clutch of photos, the sting of her hand
> across my face in one of our wars
>
> when we had grown bitter and apart.
> Some say that's the fate of the eldest daughter.[28]

As the poem continues, the memories of 'lavender polish', ordinary

details of her mother remaking an old dress or of mother and daughter
rolling wool into balls, gain immediacy and recognition.

> She'd call us in and let us skate around
> in our socks. We'd grow solemn as planets
> in an intricate orbit about her.

While the mother favours 'sensible shades: Moss Green, Mustard,
Beige', the child 'dreamt a robe of a colour/ so pure it became a word':

> I was sizing
> up the world beyond our flat patch by patch
> daily after school, and fitting each surprising
> city street to city square to diamond.

Meehan, one of Ireland's most exciting contemporary writers, voices
another side to the Demeter/Persephone story: the daughter's search for
her own space, freedom from and within the pattern.

The work of contemporary Irish women writers, such as Meehan and
the Irish-language poet Nuala Ní Dhomhnaill, provides an important
reminder of the tensions inherent in a world with strong mothers and
daughters. A discussion which omits and evades these tensions risks the
creation of further 'unspeakables'. The two sides of the mother-daughter
relationship, the potential for 'the deepest mutuality and the most painful
estrangement',[29] are expressed vividly in two poems written by Ní
Dhomhnaill. The first, titled 'Máthair',[30] is a fiercely angry poem, depths
of pain signalled by the hanging line with which the first stanza ends.

> Do thugais dom gúna
> is thógais arís é;
> do thugais dom capall
> a dhíolais i m'éagmais;
> do thugais dom cláirseach
> is d'iarrais thar n-ais é;
> do thugais dom beatha.

> [You gave me a dress
> and then took it back from me.
> You gave me a horse
> which you sold in my absence.
> You gave me a harp

and then asked me back for it.
And you gave me life.]

The daughter's breaking free from the mother requires radical action, a total separation made possible only with the killing of oneself:

dá scriosfainn an chláirseach
ag tachtadh sreanga an aoibhnis
is sreanga na beatha?

[if I broke the harp
if I choked the strings
the strings of life?]

And even at this, the mother retains the last words – 'mí-bhuíoch, scitsifréineach' (ingrate, schizophrenic).

In stark contrast, Ní Dhomhnaill's 'Dán do Mhelissa',[31] written to her daughter, dramatises a very different maternal power, the mother's wish to bestow, without restriction, all of the gifts of earth and heaven on her daughter.

Bheadh an damh ag súgradh leis an madra allta
an naíonán ag gleáchas leis an nathair nimhe,
luífeadh an leon síos leis an uan caorach
sa domhan úrnua a bhronnfainn ort mín mín.

[The ox would gambol with the wolf
the child would play with the serpent
the lion would lie down with the lamb
in the pasture world I would delicately grant.]

The mother's vision for her daughter is one of beauty and harmony, but must be phrased in the conditional tense, 'a bhronnfainn ort mín mín'. Her final declaration testifies both to the totality of the mother's protective love for her daughter and the dangers against which she may only partly succeed:

A iníon bhán, seo dearbhú ó do mháithrín
go mbeirim ar láimh duit an ghealach is an ghrian
is go seasfainn le mo chorp féin idir dhá bhró an mhuilinn
i muilte Dé chun nach meilfi tú mín mín.

> [Oh white daughter here's your mother's word:
> I will put in your hand the sun and the moon
> I will stand my body between the millstones
> in God's mills so you are not totally ground.]

Even the earliest stories of maternal love dramatise its dual nature, from Clytemnestra whose love for her daughter, Iphigenia, and her desire to avenge her betrayal by Agamemnon, make her the 'antithesis of the nurturing mother figure'.[32] In a more recent narrative, Toni Morrison's 1987 novel *Beloved*, a woman commits infanticide in order to prevent her child being brought back into slavery, seeking to protect 'her best thing, her beautiful, magical best thing – the part of her that was clean'.[33] Sethe's actions, where 'motherlove was a killer',[34] form 'unspeakable things, unspoken' until retold by Morrison's novel. In Boland's 'The Making of an Irish Goddess,' the mythical figure of Ceres, who rescues her daughter, gives way to the similarly desperate actions of historical women:

> the failed harvests,
> the fields rotting to the horizon,
> the children devoured by their mothers
> whose souls, they would have said,
> went straight to hell,
> followed by their own.[35]

Both nurturing and constricting, creative and destructive, 'motherlove' may be a 'killer'. If through Demeter, mother of Persephone, and Mary, mother of Jesus, we overcome 'the unthinkable of death by postulating maternal love in its place',[36] Boland, Morrison and Ní Dhomhnaill attest to the continuance of the 'unthinkable' within maternal love itself.

*

The ambivalence which exists within a term such as 'the spiritual strain', women writers' concern with the life of the spirit and the tensions thus uncovered, is also to be found within 'the unspeakable'. Throughout our culture, the female is associated with the unspeakable, as the realm of instinct, emotion and the body. Female images and symbols also express the unnameable in the sense of that which is transcendent – the ineffable or unutterable – yet through whom the word is made flesh. Contemporary women writers inherit this symbolic pattern, many of whom celebrate the location of a space outside or beyond words which they characterise as a distinctively female space, in Boland's words 'the silences in which are our beginnings'. Yet the association of woman and the unspeakable is also a troubling one; the *unspeakable* may cover over or obscure what is *unspoken*, what needs to be spoken.

A further, and darker, side to the unspeakable or the unutterable also exists: that which is too awful to be spoken, which approaches the unimaginable. Very often, this 'unspeakable' is embodied through female images; thus, media representations of famine and catastrophe, of break-downs which are almost unimaginable in scale and horror, choose images of mothers and children, of women unable to feed their children, of a dead child at its mother's breast. Contemporary Ireland provides further examples of how the unutterable is embodied in the lives of individual women, with the names of Anne Lovett, the girl called 'X' and others still painfully present in public memory, and yet unspeakable. In these ways, the spiritual strain for women is also a physical strain; as female images embody the unutterable of pain and suffering, there results for women a tension, even alienation from the female body.

In her conclusion to *Of Woman Born*, Adrienne Rich sets at least one agenda for the future:[37]

> In arguing that we have by no means yet explored or understood our biological grounding, the miracle and paradox of the female body and its spiritual and political meanings, I am really asking whether women cannot begin, at last, to *think through the body*, to connect what has been so cruelly disorganized – our great mental capacities, hardly used; our highly developed tactile sense; our genius for close observation; our complicated, pain-enduring, multi-pleasured physicality.

Contemporary women's writing frequently expresses the pain endured by women, of the spirit and of the body, most memorably among Irish writing in Paula Meehan's brave and heart-rending poem, 'The Statue of the Virgin at Granard speaks'.[38] The poem, voiced by Mary, expresses her longing and yearning to be 'incarnate, incarnate,/ maculate and tousled in a honeyed bed'. With the passage of the seasons, the scene moves to All Souls' Night and Mary's despair as she recalls how, 'on a night like this' she witnessed the death of a young girl 'alone at my feet':

> and though she cried out to me in extremis
> I did not move,
> I didn't lift a finger to help her,
> I didn't intercede with heaven,
> nor whisper the charmed word in God's ear.

The harrowing tones of Meehan's poem have few equivalents. One, perhaps, is Toni Morrison's challenging novel *Beloved*, a work which like Meehan attests to the 'complicated, pain-enduring' character of maternity. Yet *Beloved* is also a work which offers healing, glimpsing, through the voice of Baby Suggs, what Rich has called our 'multi-pleasured physicality'. Following in the tradition of female lay preachers, Baby Suggs, the novel's matriarchal figure, goes to 'the Clearing' to preach. In the face of the injustice and physical brutality of slavery, she delivers a passionate and unforgettable sermon of spiritual and physical survival:[39]

> 'Here,' she said, 'in this here place, we flesh; flesh that weeps, laughs; flesh that dances on bare feet in grass. Love it. Love it hard. Yonder they do not love your flesh. They despise it. They don't love your eyes; they'd just as soon pick em out. No more do they love the skin on your back. Yonder they flay it. And O my people they do not love your hands. Those they only use, tie, bind, chop off and leave empty. Love your hands! Love them. Raise them up and kiss them. Touch others with them, pat them together, stroke them on your face 'cause they don't love that either. *You* got to love it, *you!* ... The dark, dark liver – love it, love it, and the beat and beating heart, love that too. More than eyes or feet. More than lungs that have yet to draw free air. More than your life-holding womb and your life-giving private parts, hear me now, love your heart. For this is the prize.'

Contemporary women's writings, as the above extracts demonstrate, bear witness to experiences, many of which previously were unspoken. Exploring the various strains of the 'unspeakable', love and its terrible consequence, death and its negation, writers such as Eavan Boland, Alice Walker, Nuala Ní Dhomhnaill, Paula Meehan and Toni Morrison answer the plea of generations of readers, to

> make us human
> in cadences of change and mortal pain
> and words we can grow old and die in.[40]

NOTES

1 Eavan Boland, 'Time and Violence', *In a Time of Violence* (Manchester, 1994), pp. 49-50.

2 Alice Walker, 'Saving the Life That is Your Own', *In Search of Our Mothers' Gardens* (San Diego, 1967), p. 9.

3 A. Walker, 'In Search of Our Mothers' Gardens', *In Search of Our Mothers' Gardens* (San Diego, 1967), p. 233.

4 A. Walker (see n. 2), pp. 7, 13.

5 For a discussion of these two schools of feminist criticism, see Toril Moi, *Sexual/Textual Politics: Feminist Literary Theory* (London and New York, 1985), and Elaine Showalter, 'Feminist Criticism in the Wilderness', *Critical Inquiry* (1981), vol. 8.1, pp. 179-205.

6 Margaret Homans, *Bearing the Word: Language and Female Experience in Nineteenth-Century Women's Writing* (Chicago, 1986), xii.

7 Ibid., xi.

8 Ibid., p. 2; Homans in turn cites the work of Christine Froula on Milton's 'Paradise Lost' and Luce Irigaray's discussion of the Clytemnestra myth.

9 For a useful discussion of Lacanian theory, see Terry Eagleton, *Literary Theory: An Introduction* (Minneapolis, 1983), pp. 161-79. As Eagleton summarises (p.168), 'To enter language is to be severed from what Lacan calls the "real", that inaccessible realm which is always beyond the reach of signification, always outside the symbolic order. In particular, we are severed from the mother's body: after the Oedipus crisis, we will never be able to attain this precious object, even though we will spend all our lives hunting for it.'

10 E. Boland, 'Envoi', *Selected Poems* (1989), pp. 89-90.

11 E. Boland, 'The Journey', *Selected Poems* (Manchester, 1989), pp. 86-9.

12 Augustine Martin, 'Quest and Vision: *The Journey*', *Irish University Review* (1993), vol. 23.1, p. 84.

13 E. Boland, 'Fever', *Selected Poems* (1989), pp. 77-8.

14 E. Boland, 'Anna Liffey', *In a Time of Violence* (1994), pp. 41-6.

15 E. Boland, 'The Making of an Irish Goddess', *Outside History* (Manchester, 1990), pp. 31-2.

16 E. Boland, 'Suburban Woman: a Detail', *Selected Poems* (1989), pp. 81-2.

17 Adrienne Rich, *Of Woman Born: Motherhood as Experience and Institution* (London, 1976), p. 237.

18 For a fuller discussion of this myth, see Cathy M. Davidson and E.M. Broner (eds.), *The Lost Tradition: Mothers and Daughters in Literature* (New York, 1980), pp. 9-10, and A. Rich, op. cit., pp. 237-40.

19 A. Rich, op. cit., p. 237.

20 Ibid., p. 238.

21 Ibid., p. 240.

22 E. Boland, 'The Pomegranate', *In a Time of Violence* (1994), pp. 20-21.

23 A. Rich, op. cit., p. 225.
24 Virginia Woolf, *A Room of One's Own* (1929, London, 1977) p. 83.
25 A. Walker, (see n. 3), p.237.
26 Ibid., p. 241.
27 Ibid., p. 243.
28 Paula Meehan, 'The Pattern', *The Man Who Was Marked by Winter* (Dublin, 1991), pp. 17-20.
29 A. Rich, op. cit., p. 226.
30 Nuala Ní Dhomhnaill, 'Máthair', *Selected Poems: Rogha Dánta* (Dublin, 1991), pp. 40-1. The translations are by Michael Hartnett.
31 N. Ní Dhomhnaill, 'Dán do Mhelissa', *Selected Poems: Rogha Dánta* (1991), pp. 136-7.
32 Ida H. Washington and Carol E. Washington Tobol, 'Kriemhild and Clytemnestra', in C.M. Davidson and E.M. Broner (op. cit.), pp. 15-21.
33 Toni Morrison, *Beloved* (London, 1987), p. 251.
34 Ibid., p. 132.
35 E. Boland, 'The Making of an Irish Goddess', *Outside History* (1990), pp. 31-2.
36 Julia Kristeva, 'Stabat Mater', in Toril Mori (ed.), *Julia Kristeva Reader* (Oxford, 1986), p. 176.
37 A. Rich, op. cit., p. 284.
38 P. Meehan, 'The Statue of the Virgin at Granard Speaks', *The Man Who Was Marked by Winter* (1991), pp. 40-2.
39 T. Morrison, op. cit., pp. 88-9.
40 E. Boland, 'Time and Violence', *In a Time of Violence* (1994), pp. 49-50.

Sounds Sacred: Immanence and Transcendence in Music[1]

ANNE M. MURPHY

> All good art and literature begin in immanence. But
> they do not stop there ...
> It is the enterprise and privilege of the aesthetic to
> quicken into lit presence the continuum between
> temporality and eternity.
>
> George Steiner[2]

DEFINING TERMS

The title of this essay is open to a number of interpretations. For instance, 'Sounds Sacred' might be an abbreviated form of '*It* sounds sacred' where 'it' is a melody, a piece of music, a combination of instruments or voices, or even a mood evoked; 'Sounds Sacred', would, in this sense then, suggest the evocation of a religious context. Alternatively, 'Sounds Sacred' might be a category title from a contemporary CD listings, where the ellipted 'Sounds [that are] Sacred' is intended to be more alluring than the potentially rather staid and familiar labels such as Religious Music or Sacred Music, for example.

There is no correct or incorrect interpretation of the title. It is intended merely to suggest an openness, or a connection between sound(s) and sacredness. This connection is the object of investigation in the present paper and is suggested in the subtitle: *Immanence and Transcendence in Music.*

Immanence and transcendence are traditional terms from philosophical and theological discourse. The concepts of immanence and transcendence are commonly defined in terms of, and in relation to, one another. For instance, one influential dictionary definition of immanence[3] contrasts it with transcendence as meaning that which does not exceed a limit. The corollary, therefore, is that transcendence is the *surpassing* of a limit. Transcendence pertains to the realm of the metaphysical; it is an attribute beyond the finite range of human experience and the confines of the material universe.

71

This article extends the application of the terms immanence and transcendence from philosophical and theological discourse into musical discourse. It offers an immanence- and transcendence-based approach to musical investigation which, it will be shown, provides a framework for a revelatory model of analysis. This model conveys the notion of an epistemology of music which takes into account not only all that belongs to the sense-experience of music, that is its immanence or immanent data, but also recognises its *transcendence*.

INTRODUCING THE MODEL

The transcendent dimension of music, as explained above, is seen here as that aspect of music which embraces all that belongs to the realisation of the distinctive elements of rhythm, melody and harmony and which cannot be contained within the limits of verifiable data. Using Example 1 below, for instance, we can demonstrate how transcendent beauty in music derives from apparently rather economical musical means. The example illustrates a musical formula consisting of eight melodic figures, where the chosen Key (or series of notes related to a keynote or tonal centre) is E flat: [See Example 1 on next page]

These eight figures form the substance of the Sanctus, from Gabriel Fauré's *Requiem*. At a basic level of data deconstruction, they might be seen as the core elements from which the overall musical structure derives. If we were interested in designing a Fauré pastiche, we might well be in a position to suggest a set of rules or commands, in the manner of a computer program, which would generate those core elements and modify them to dictate the particular musical texture of the piece. Using the *Sanctus* as the model, four steps are necessary for such a generation:

1   Adaptation or organisation of the melodic figures according to a rhythmic pattern of three beats to a measure or bar [3/4 time signature].

2   Allocation of the melodic lines, mostly antiphonally, to female and male voices, having them sing in harmony only on the last note.

3   Underpinning of the whole melodic and rhythmic structure with appropriate (broken) chords to support the voices.

EXAMPLE I

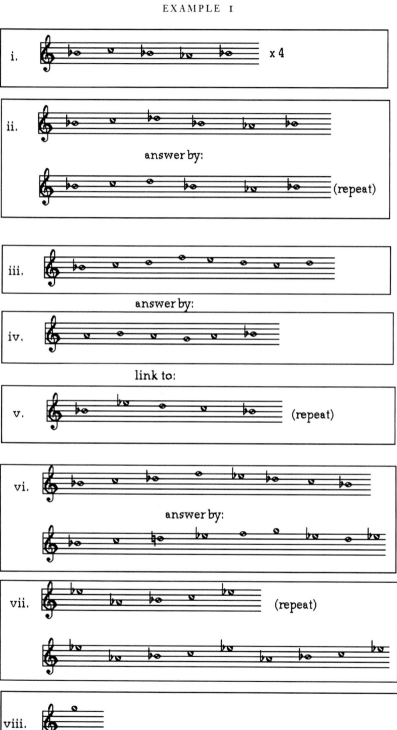

4 Orchestration with strings and harp and the addition of a counter
melody played by a solo violin; occasional introduction of some brass
instruments to evoke a mood as well as to match and illuminate the
chosen text.

Clearly, the precise manner in which the elements of any piece of music
are created and modified is dictated by a range of factors, such as the
appropriate setting of a liturgical text, for example. Neverthless, the 4-
step process illustrated here for Fauré's *Sanctus* indicates one means of
capturing the technical details behind the music.

The immanence of the technical data is a poor indication of the transcendent experience which is offered by this incense-laden *Sanctus*. But
how can one explain the distance between the above analysis and the
experience of the music itself? All good art begins in immanence,
Steiner claims, but it does not stop there.

It would be interesting to speculate on how such apparent frugality
of musical elements is capable of achieving such glorious confection of
sound and transcendent beauty. Perhaps the appeal is to some ill-defined
aspect of the senses, or even to our spiritual sensibilities. However, it is
the *theological* dimension underlying composition which will be considered in detail here. The discussion which follows attempts to explore
this theological dimension, or what we shall call the 'lit presence'
between the temporality of music and its intimations of eternity.

The *Sanctus* is God-centred and is divine praise in its purest form. It
is the only movement of the Requiem Mass which does not refer to the
dead or to our petitions on their behalf. Furthermore, the *Benedictus*, the
second part of this hymn of praise which echoes the praise given to
Christ, God made Man, upon his triumphal entry into Jerusalem, is not
included. The context of this praise is totally celestial. However, the
musical setting subtly draws our attention in another direction – towards
those who *offer* this praise and petition. This is achieved by means of
the solo violin's counter-melody which reproduces the soprano melody
of the opening movement, the *Introit: Requiem aeternam dona eis Domine.*
The counter-melody echoes the Introit's petitions to the Lord God in
Sion for eternal rest and light for the departed:

> *Te decet hymnus, Deus in Sion. ... exaudi, exaudi orationem, ad te*
> *omnis caro veniet.*

One one level, the music of the *Sanctus* evokes the infinite holiness of
the deity. On another, however, it is the accessibility of God which is

emphasised. The counter-melody, with its allusion to the first movement, reminds us that all flesh can come to God (*ad te omnis caro veniet*)
who will not remain deaf to our pleading. The God of this *Sanctus* is
not wholly Other, but within reach of our need. In the following section,
we will examine the means by which composers, or artists, have conveyed aspects of the 'lit presence' described above.

THE ARTIST AND THE PROPHET

For the purposes of this paper, the consideration of immanence and
transcendence in music is based on a theory of connectedness between
music, meaning and mystery, and between spirituality and art. The
existence of a spiritual, religious and theological dimension of art has
been commented on by George Steiner:

> The gravity and constancy at the heart of major forms and of our
> understanding of them are religious in [that they] enact ... a root
> impulse of the human spirit to explore possibilities of meaning
> and of truth that lie outside empirical seizure or proof.[4]

Further, Karl Rahner has stated that the adjective 'religious', in a broad
sense, is applicable to all that 'gives concrete expression to [woman's
and] man's infinite transcendence'.[5] The acceptance of this definition
allows us to infer that every instance of such transcendence has a religious dimension. In this broad sense, human nature, by virtue of its
innate creativity, may be said to be religious. Human creativity, as the
expression of hope, needs and desires, witnesses to that instinct within
the human spirit which energises women and men to see beyond the
limitations of temporal existence and to rise above them. Human creativity is a statement of belief that life is meaningful. Human creativity is a
statement of hope; it concretises in sign and symbol, word and image, the
human craving for permanence and value, a craving in fact for immortality.

The creative artist has always been at the forefront of the search for
meaning and significance. It is, perhaps, the vocation of the artist to
express this searching dimension of being human. The creative artist is
the spokesperson, often unawares, whose art can offer to fellow human
beings a perspective on the ultimate questions of life and death.
Through his or her giftedness, the artist becomes the prophet and
visionary whose art evidences what David Tracy calls 'the instinct for
the essential'.[6]

This 'essential' embodies some grain of eternal truth and beauty and, as such, has a 'disclosive and transformative power' for all those who experience it.[7] This is the hallmark of greatness and value in art. The work of art, therefore, whatever its medium or form, is a concretisation of the transcendent dimension of human nature. It gives validity, authenticity and credibility to the possible easing and eventual resolution of all conflict and yearning.

THE MYSTERY OF MUSIC AS LANGUAGE

It is something of a mystery that the precise and scientifically verifiable phenomena of musical language – for example, the pitches, durations, timbres and dynamic values – should, in combination, be capable of moving the listener in a way that is beyond that which is measurable either in terms of technical expertise or intellectual understanding. That music can and does move us in this way is beyond dispute; *how* it does so is less easily definable. It has been said that 'Music is a code in which the deepest secrets of humanity are written.'[8] This makes of music at once a mysterious language and the language of mystery.

Such terms as mystery, meaning and essence are somewhat nebulous. But the creative artist, however tangible the raw materials of the art, belongs in this territory where shadow and substance interact. The composer whose music analysts attempt to understand, is something of a visionary and a prophet gifted with that instinct for the 'essential' of which David Tracy speaks. Consciously or unconsciously, the creative artist is engaged in the revelation of meaning through his/her art form, and walks constantly in the realms of mystery, - the mysteries of the art, life and religion with which art in all its forms is so engaged. As Leibnitz stated:

> music is a secret arithmetic of the soul unknowing of the fact that it is counting.[9]

In an attempt to illuminate some of this theoretical material, this arithmetic, let us consider the musical potential and compositional possibilities inherent in a single note. To paraphrase that resounding cliché about the longest journey beginning with a single step, the keynote – or the chord on the keynote – is the starting point for even the most gargantuan tonal symphony.

For example, we might consider the possibilities, or the musical potential, for the note A in the second space of the treble stave. It is the note to which orchestras tune and whose frequency of vibration, 440 cycles per second, constitutes what is known as concert pitch. As a single sound, it may be realised in a range of ways. For instance, it may occur as a long sustained note suggesting serenity, a resting place or an ending. In this case, it may provide an appropriate musical painting of words such as, *still, peace,* or *rest,* for example. If the A occurs in rhythmic groupings determined by accent placement, it may convey waltz time (where the accent is on the first of three notes) or march time (the first of fours notes), or jig time (the first of six notes), for example. Melodically, the A may act as the starting point or home note of a series or group of notes, i.e. **d r m f s - f m r d**, where the 'doh' is the A. Harmonically, A may act as a member of a chord or group of notes which may be sounded simultaneously, i.e. **d m s**. In this context of a triad or three-note chord, the character or tonal colouring of the A will vary according to whether it is the **root** or foundation of that chord (A C/Csharp E), the **third/** middle/ or filling note of the musical sandwich or the **fifth** or upper note of the triad. There are, of course, many other ways in which the musical potential of A might be realised. Some obvious development strategies might include deviations of pitch, either melodically or harmonically, dynamic changes, and the natural changes of timbre whereby the tonal quality of the note is dictated by the instrument or voice on which it is produced.

At this point, however, we wish to trace a real musical journey of A. The context is the opening 17 bars of the Introit of Fauré's *Requiem,* and the text is:

> *Requiem aeternam dona eis Domine*
> Eternal rest give unto them O Lord; and let perpetual light shine upon them.

The opening word REQUIEM/REST is the key to the mood of the opening which is one of serene and unhurried but insistent prayer of petition. It has something of the character of a recitative in its unadorned and starkly accompanied style. A single low unison D calls in the voices. The repeated A of the sopranos is the fifth or top of the triad on D, and the other voices support it in the minor mode of the triad. The movement is moulded by the rhythm of the words. The long-breathed accompanying D which underpins the harmonic structure and the static melodic content evokes a sense of timelessness which befits a setting of *aeternam* /eternal. The first relief from this trance-like state comes on the word *Domine* /Lord. There is a downward movement in

the accompaniment after *aeternam* and the soprano A becomes the
springboard for an appropriate rise of pitch for *Domine*. The A is still
present, but it is now in the alto line and is the third, or filling of the
chord. The downward accompaniment is reflected, mirror-like in the
rising soprano melody whose high point is reached in the phrase:

et lux perpetua

The continuation of this light is suggested by repetition of the word
*luceat/*shine in a downward curving series of steps. At its lowest point,
the series, turning through subtly altering chordal combinations and
shadings, draws the melody back to repeated A, making it eventually
come to rest as the root of the bright dominant chord of A major. The
effect is that of suffusing the close of this opening section in a gentle,
optimistic light. The music, both technically and emotionally, has
reached a point at which the ear anticipates the return to the opening
key and the mind and heart are eased by a more lyrical and extended
setting of the text of the *Requiem aeternam*.

It is beyond the scope of this paper to offer a detailed analysis of
every technical aspect of the section which follows. Nevertheless, it is
important to highlight the following elements, since they play a crucial
role in forming the texture of the piece and, as such, should be the
focus for critical listening:

a) the melody hovers between the tonic chord of D minor and the
chord of A in its major and minor mode;

b) a rising curve of the chord of D minor is suggestive both of light [*et
lux* fig. C] and of petition [*dona* fig. D];[10]

c) the lyrical middle section in B flat reaches its climax [fig. F] in the
repeated pleas to *hear hear our prayer/exaudi, exaudi orationem* ...;

d) a rising chromatic chord heightens the tension before the emotion
subsides in six bars of irresistible beauty and simplicity reminding
the petitioned deity of the need and trusting approach of all humanity: *ad te omnis caro veniet*. Technically also the music reaches the sta-
bility and optimism of the dominant A major chord which comes to
rest within the chord of D minor which ushers in the final section
[*Kyrie eleison* fig. G.].

e) The *Kyrie eleison* is a contracted reprise of material from the lyrical setting of *Requiem aeternam* earlier in the movement. The most noteworthy feature of this section is the triple repetition of *eleison* using the three notes F, E, {E flat}, D until the movement comes to rest as it began on a unison note D.

No amount of analytical detail can explain the distance between this complex mix of technical data and the mysterious chemistry whereby that data speaks to the human spirit of transcendent realities. These realities which are at once beyond us, yet strangely part of us.

MUSIC AS A THEOPHANY

Steiner has observed that '[Music] has long been, it continues to be, the unwritten theology of those who lack or reject any formal creed'.[11] The *Requiem* of Fauré is just one example of an unwritten theology which offers an epiphany of hope and meaning which is beyond 'immanence and verification'.[12] This is a theophany transcending considerations of formal faith or culture. The experience of it is like that of Job who heard His 'songs in the night'. It allows us to touch the hem of the eternal.

But how does music communicate and move us to such deep emotion and feeling? It is possible merely to suggest briefy some means here. Music would seem to communicate through its rhythmic patterns which have been drawn from the subconscious rhythmic impulses of biological or natural life. It would seem to communicate through the rise and fall of its melodies, attempting to pattern the movements of exaltation and despair which express the strength and the weakness of the human spirit. It would seem to communicate through the conflict and concord of sounds which resonate with the bitter sweetness of life experience. Through all of these elements music communicates. Its communication is not exact, rather is it associative. This communication in both its process and in its objective association is strongly redolent of mystery. In this would appear to lie its power, its universality, its timeless appeal.

'Serious music, art, literature, in their own wager on survivance, are refusals of analytic-empirical criteria of constraint' and are beyond immanence and verification.[13] They suggest that in our humanity, for all our faults and weaknesses there is, as Steinbeck describes it, 'a shining'.

I would like to close this paper by letting music itself be the most compelling witness to its own transcendent dimension. The *Agnus Dei* from Fauré's *Requiem* contains a particularly shining passage which will illuminate my efforts to articulate something of the mysterious process whereby the immanent data of music is transformed into an expression of the most profound longings of our restless human spirit.

The *Pie Jesu* for treble solo is the central movement of Fauré's *Requiem*. After this tranquil oasis of limpid beauty, the colours darken in the triple invocation of the *Agnus Dei*. There is an arc of rogational intensity which rises to a still point of expectancy poised on a single dominant note on the word *lux*. For two timeless bars we wait, alert to every nuance in this thread of sound. As the word *lux* gives way to *aeternam* the tension dissipates in the glowing warmth of a full chord. The movement draws to a close bathed in a radiant confidence that prayer has been heard, darkness has given way to eternal light, and, because the Lord is good, the souls of the departed are at rest forever.

NOTES

1 The application of an immanence and transcendence-based approach to musical analysis can only be fully appreciated by detailed listening to the works cited.

2 *Real Presences* (London, 1989), p. 227.

3 Karl Rahner and Herbert Vorgrimler, 'Religion', *Concise Theological Dictionary* 2nd ed., (London, 1983), p. 229.

4 George Steiner, op. cit., p. 225.

5 Karl Rahner and Herbert Vorgrimler, op. cit., p. 437. The broad understanding of such terms as 'belief', 'faith', 'religion', which pertains throughout this paper can be supported, to a large extent, by the writings of many contemporary theologians, primarily Karl Rahner. Cf. 'Faith', *Encyclopaedia of Theology*, ed. Karl Rahner (London, 1975); 'Christianity and the Non-Christian Religions', and 'Christology within an Evolutionary View of the World', in *Theological Investigations* 5 (1966), 115-34 and 157-92.

6 David Tracy, *The Analogical Imagination: Christian Theology and the Culture of Pluralism* (London, 1981), p. 110.

7 David Tracy, op. cit.

8 Nicholas Cook, *A Guide to Musical Analysis* (London, 1987), p. 1.

9 Quoted by George Steiner, op. cit., p. 217.

10 The figuration in this section refers to the vocal score of the Fauré Requiem aranged by Desmond Ratcliffe, Novello (1975).

11 George Steiner, op. cit., p. 218.

12 Ibid., 229.

13 Ibid., pp. 225-6.

Spirituality Reflected in the Visual Arts

EILEEN KANE

The word 'spirituality', understood in its broadest sense, refers, as we know, to the life of the spirit, that is, spirit as opposed to matter. But it has also the meaning of 'that which is concerned with sacred or religious things'. It is in that sense that it is used here. This paper considers how sets of ideas concerning spirituality in the context of the Christian faith are reflected in the visual arts.

As the centuries pass and artistic styles change, so do the aspects of Christian spirituality which come into visual focus. Further, Christian spirituality itself may vary in its emphasis and consequently in its visual expression not only from generation to generation but also, within any given generation, according to the personality of an individual or a community. So, at any given date, and even in the same country, widely divergent aspects, even kinds of spirituality, within the one Christian tradition, may find expression in architecture, painting and sculpture as well as in the decorative arts.

There are memorable moments in the history of art, when divergent views and various aspects of spirituality find visual expression in works which are monuments not only of art but also of spirituality. One such moment occurs in the twelfth century, another in the fifteenth. In the twelfth century, the moment is created by two Churchmen, St Bernard of Clairvaux and Abbot Suger of Saint-Denis. In the fifteenth, it occurs in the work of two painters, Roger van der Weyden and Fra Angelico.

SAINT BERNARD AND ABBOT SUGER

Bernard of Clairvaux and Abbot Suger of Saint-Denis were contemporaries: Suger died in 1151, at the age of 70, while Bernard died two years later, still in his sixties. Both were French; both were monks. In terms of spirituality, however, they occupy very different positions. We can be certain of each man's views on art and spirituality, because each wrote them down. Neither man was an artist, but each was, in his own way, a patron of the arts, in the sense that he caused art to be created,

81

and the imprint of each can be seen especially in the architecture of his time.

When we consider Bernard of Clairvaux, we think of him as a contemplative, a man of prayer. That, he surely was, but he was also a man of action, a preacher, a reformer of monastic life.[1] Some, at least, of the influence he exercised, came through his writings – letters, sermons, treatises. It is in one of his letters, the *Apologia to William of St Thierry*,[2] written in 1125, that we can read his views on art in relation to spirituality. These views are already quite well known, but it is instructive to examine them afresh, in the context in which they were first expressed.[3]

In the *Apologia*, Bernard is fulminating against the laxity which, as he saw it, had crept into monastic life as lived in the great Benedictine abbey of Cluny, in his own native Burgundy, and in its affiliated houses. He denounces various excesses and abuses in the day-to-day life of the monks, various departures from the monastic Rule, infidelities to the way of poverty as a value central to the religious life. 'I am astonished,' he writes, 'that monks could be so lacking in moderation in matters of food and drink, and with respect to clothing and bedding, carriages and buildings.'[4] 'How absurd,' he exclaims. 'Great care is taken to see that the body is clothed according to the Rule, whilst the Rule is broken by leaving the soul naked. A good deal of attention is given to getting a robe and cowl for the body, since a man is not reckoned a monk without them. Meanwhile there is no thought for his spiritual attire, the spirit of prayer and humility.'[5] Bernard's prime emphasis, therefore, is on priorities, and specifically on the priorities of the monastic life: prayer, (that is, contemplative prayer), humility, poverty and charity.

With these priorities in mind, and remembering especially that Bernard was addressing himself specifically to monks, we read what he has to say, in the last part of his letter, about monastic buildings – churches, cloisters – and their decoration.

> I shall say nothing about the soaring heights and extravagant lengths and unnecessary widths of the churches, nothing about their expensive decorations and their novel images, which catch the attention of those who go in to pray, and dry up their devotion ... However, as one monk to another, may I ask the question which a heathen poet put to his fellows. 'Tell me, O priests,' he said, 'why is there gold in the holy place?' I shall put the question slightly differently ... 'Tell me, O poor men – if you are really poor men – why is there gold in the holy place?' It is not the same for monks and bishops. Bishops have a duty toward both wise and foolish.

They have to make use of material ornamentation to rouse devotion in a carnal people, incapable of spiritual things. But we no longer belong to such people. For the sake of Christ we have abandoned all the world holds valuable and attractive. All that is beautiful in sight and sound and scent we have left behind, all that is pleasant to taste and touch ... Therefore, I ask you, can it be our own devotion we are trying to excite with such display, or is the purpose of it to win the admiration of fools and the offerings of simple folk? ... Let me speak plainly. Cupidity, which is a form of idolatry, is the cause of all this. It is for no useful purpose that we do it, but to attract gifts ... The very sight of such sumptuous and exquisite baubles is sufficient to inspire men to make offerings, though not to say their prayers ... Oh, vanity of vanities, whose vanity is rivalled only by its insanity! The walls of the church are aglow, but the poor of the Church go hungry. The stones of the church are covered with gold, while its children are left naked. The food of the poor is taken to feed the eyes of the rich, and amusement is provided for the curious, while the needy have not even the necessities of life'.

Bernard finally asks: 'What excuse can there be for these ridiculous monstrosities in the cloisters where the monks do their reading, extraordinary things at once beautiful and ugly? Here we find filthy monkeys and fierce lions, fearful centaurs, harpies, and striped tigers, soldiers at war, and hunters blowing their horns ... All round there is such an amazing variety of shapes that one could easily prefer to take one's reading from the walls instead of from a book. One could spend the whole day gazing fascinated at these things, one by one, instead of meditating on the law of God ...'[6]

Very little remains to-day of that great abbey or of its church, but the scholarly reconstruction of the final version of it by Professor Kenneth John Conant, demonstrates clearly how Bernard could have been moved to use the words he did: 'Soaring heights and extravagant lengths and unnecessary widths'.[7] Built between, about, 1086 and 1147, the abbey church measured more than 187 metres in length,[8] comparable only with St Peter's in Rome.

The monkeys and lions, centaurs, harpies and striped tigers that Bernard would banish from his monastery, may indeed be found, if not all together in one great company, at least in ones and twos carved on the capitals of columns in churches, chapels and cloisters all over Romanesque France and beyond. The nave of the pilgrimage church of

St Mary Magdalen at Vézelay, also in Burgundy, is distinguished both architecturally and sculpturally. The church was building between 1120, date of a disastrous fire in the pre-existing church and adjoining monastery, and 1138. Bernard certainly knew Vézelay, and he would preach the second crusade from the northern slope of the hill there, in March 1146. Could he have already seen the marvellous capital on one of the columns in the nave, on which is carved the figure of St Hubert as a huntsman, blowing his horn as he gallops along on his horse, his cloak flying out behind him?[9]

On the other hand, the simplicity of the architecture and the extreme restraint of the carved decoration in the abbey church of Fontenay, founded by Saint Bernard in a wooded valley in Burgundy in 1118, proclaim a spirituality of interiority, detachment from worldly attractions, avoidance of the lure of wealth. The shadowy, windowless nave leads to the choir, or sanctuary, at its east end. There the light pours in through five large windows. It is a visual reflection of that process by which the soul moves out of its own darkness towards the light of the presence of God. Similarly, at Pontigny, near Auxerre, there is created an atmosphere of serenity and of calm which is conducive to contemplative prayer, again, surely, a reflection in the art of architecture of the spirituality of St Bernard and, more generally, of the Cistercian monks.[10]

St Bernard, then, represents one point of view: the simplicity, interiority, poverty and austerity of the monastic life. Abbot Suger, on the other hand, was working in a quite different context. From 1122 until his death, on 13 January 1151, he was abbot of the ancient and royal abbey of Saint-Denis, not far outside Paris. At Saint-Denis were kept the relics of the first bishop of Paris, martyred with his companions, Rusticus and Eleutherius, in 250. It was the burial place of the kings of France, and had custody of the royal regalia, used at the king's coronation, and, in times of peace, of the *Oriflamme*, the banner fetched by the king at the commencement of war. It was far from being a place where one might come to find solitude or to practise humility or poverty of spirit.

Suger's views on the subject of art and spirituality are almost diametrically opposed to those of St Bernard. Where Bernard sought to express the ideal of personal poverty and humility of life by creating a simple, undecorated, unworldly setting for contemplative prayer, Suger's desire was to use whatever was most precious in the world which God had created, in order to give glory to God. Suger celebrates Creation. For him, the material things of this earth serve to lead the mind and heart upwards to the immaterial, to what is not of this earth. The glory of this earth is, for him, an analogy of the glory of heaven. It allows him, while dwelling on this earth, to contemplate the glory of God's dwelling-place in heaven. So, to Bernard's question: 'Why is there gold in the holy place?', Suger would answer:

> To me ... one thing has always seemed preeminently fitting: that every costlier or costliest thing should serve, first and foremost, for the administration of the Holy Eucharist. *If* golden pouring vessels, golden vials, golden little mortars used to serve, by the word of God or the command of the Prophet, to collect the *blood of goats or calves or the red heifer: how much more* must golden vessels, precious stones, and whatever is most valued among all created things, be laid out, with continual reverence and full devotion, for the reception of the blood of Christ! ... We profess that we must do homage also through the outward ornaments of sacred vessels, and to nothing in the world in an equal degree as to the service of the Holy Sacrifice, with all inner purity and with all outward splendor.[11]

Suger was born in 1081 and entered Saint-Denis as an oblate at the age of nine or ten. He received part of his education at Saint-Benoît-sur-Loire, but spent most of his life at Saint-Denis, whose history he has come to dominate. He achieved wide recognition as a man of wisdom and learning, became the friend, confidant and adviser of two kings of France, Louis VI 'le Gros', and Louis VII, and was appointed Regent of France during the second crusade (1147-9).[12] During his abbacy of Saint-Denis, Suger undertook the reconstruction of the abbey church, and renewed and refurbished the splendid decoration of the altar and the sacred furnishings. Although the rebuilding of the abbey church was not completed during his lifetime,[13] he put his own imprint on it, and was able to set down in two books entitled, one *De Administratione* and the other *De Consecratione*, what he had done concerning the remodelling and redecoration and, with an account of the solemn consecration, on 11 June 1144, what his ideas and intentions had been.

Suger's own words, which he caused to be cast in verse on the great bronze doors of the central portal of the abbey church give an insight into his ideas on art and spirituality:

> Whoever thou art, if thou seekest to extol the glory of these doors,

Marvel not at the gold and the expense but at the craftsmanship
   of the work.
Bright is the noble work; but, being nobly bright, the work

Should brighten the minds, so that they may travel, through the
   true lights,
To the True Light where Christ is the true door.
In what manner it be inherent in this world the golden door
   defines:
The dull mind rises to truth through that which is material
And, in seeing this light, is resurrected from its former
   submersion.[14]

So, God is the true light, and Christ is the true door. We can see how
analogy and symbol are important for Suger. In that symbolism, light
was at the centre. Because God is light, therefore light, for Suger, symbolised and referred to God himself. Suger not only wrote about light in
this way, he also saw to it that the idea found visual expression in the
architecture itself, for, as one enters the abbey church of Saint-Denis,
passing through the great west doors and through a shadowy ante-nave,
the raised choir at the east end appears flooded in brilliant light. The
choir is surrounded by a double ambulatory, which Suger described as a
'circular string of chapels, by virtue of which the whole [church] would
shine with the wonderful and uninterrupted light of the most luminous
windows, pervading the inner beauty'.[15] Suger, further, filled those windows with stained glass, of which some still survives, notably the
window of the Tree of Jesse, which began the series. These windows,
too, were part of his plan to use art in the service of spirituality, by
'urging us onward', as he wrote, 'from the material to the immaterial'.[16]
   The quality of Suger's spirituality, its depth, its fervour and the joy
which pervaded it, are made manifest in that passage in the De
Administratione where he writes of the 'Main Altar of the blessed
Denis' and its decoration:

Often we contemplate, out of sheer affection for the church our
mother, these different ornaments both new and old; ... then I
say, sighing deeply in my heart: *Every precious stone was thy cover-
ing, the sardius, the topaz, and the jasper, the chrysolite, and the
onyx, and the beryl, the sapphire, and the carbuncle, and the emer-
ald.*[17] To those who know the properties of precious stones it
becomes evident, to their utter astonishment, that none is absent

from the number of these (with the only exception of the carbuncle), but that they abound most copiously. Thus, when – out of my delight in the beauty of the house of God – the loveliness of the many-coloured gems has called me away from external cares, and worthy meditation has induced me to reflect, transferring that which is material to that which is immaterial, on the diversity of the sacred virtues: then it seems to me that I see myself dwelling, as it were, in some strange region of the universe which neither exists entirely in the slime of the earth nor entirely in the purity of Heaven; and that, by the grace of God, I can be transported from this inferior to that higher world in an anagogical manner.[18]

Bernard and Suger, then, have given us two written texts in which ideas concerning spirituality are set out in language which is compelling to read. And those same ideas find visual expression in works of art whose power over the spectator is no less compelling than the written word.

ROGER VAN DER WEYDEN AND FRA ANGELICO

Bernard and Suger, compatriots and churchmen, were, if not close friends, very well acquainted with one another.[19] In the case of the painters Roger van der Weyden (1399/1400-64) and Fra Angelico (?1387-1455), we cannot be sure that they were personally acquainted, though there is evidence in the work of Roger, after a visit he made to Italy in the Holy Year of 1450, that he had at least seen some of the paintings of Angelico in Florence. Like Bernard and Suger, these two men also were contemporaries, and they represent two quite different facets of Christian spirituality. Though neither man committed to writing his thoughts on art and spirituality, or even on art itself, we can be sure that each of them was deeply spiritual.[20] Their texts are their paintings.

Roger van der Weyden painted the *Descent from the Cross* (fig. 1), now in the Museo del Prado, Madrid, for the chapel of the Archers' guild in the church of Notre-Dame-hors-les-Murs at Louvain in about 1435 or 1436.[21] He shows the body of Christ, taken down from the cross, and about to be placed in the arms of his mother. She, however, has fainted with grief, and has fallen into a posture which almost exactly repeats that of her son. She is tended by St John and by one of the other Maries. Their faces reflect both grief – for Christ – and tender caring – for his mother. Behind St John, another of the holy women presses the cloth of

1 Roger van der Weyden, *Descent from the Cross*, Prado, Madrid

her veil against her eyes, as her tears course down her cheeks. Over on
the far side of the cross, Mary Magdalen wrings her hands as she contemplates the wounds in Christ's feet. The intensity of the grief shown
by all the people represented is almost unbearable. To concentrate the
tension and the emotion even further, Roger denies us the possibility of
escape. With the figures in the scene, we the spectators are locked into
the box-like space which Roger has created, leaving only a narrow strip
of ground on which the participants in the drama may stand. We are
uncomfortably close to all this grief.

What strikes us most forcefully in this work is the emotivity, the
intensity of feeling which Roger conveys. But, within that, what is
emphasised is the humanity of Christ. There is nothing glorious about
him, and nothing intellectual or abstract about the picture as a whole. It
is real. All of it is real. These figures are real, and their emotion is real.
This is our world, our grief, our experience.

Not much later in date than the Prado painting, is a *Lamentation over
the Body of Christ*, in the Musées Royaux des Beaux-Arts de Belgique, at
Brussels.[22] Here there is greater simplicity than in the Prado picture,
greater concentration, but even greater intensity. The moment por-

trayed, in the history of Christ's life, is close in time to that in the *Descent from the Cross*, but the emphasis has changed. What matters here is love – Christ's love for us, for whom he chose to die, so that we might live; Mary's love for her son, whose body, now rigid in death, she tearfully embraces; the 'beloved disciple', John's love for Christ whose body he supports, while, gently, he places a caring hand on the head of his now adoptive mother; the Magdalen's love for Christ, at whose feet, her traditional place, she kneels, remembering how she had already washed them with her tears. Roger has given us some space here, but it does not relieve the tension. Rather, it participates in it, with the bleakness of the landscape, the dead tree, the foot of the cross, the skull. This is a world in which nothing matters but Christ, and his love.

Other paintings by Roger van der Weyden could be cited in which the humanity of Christ is emphasised. The *Miraflores Altarpiece*, for instance (Berlin, Stiftung Preussischer Kulturbesitz, Staatliche Museen), consists of three panels, in each of which Christ's relationship with his mother at a critical moment of his life is explored: in his infancy, after his death and after his Resurrection. In this altarpiece, it is the meaning, more than the emotion, which matters. Also, tiny subsidiary scenes are introduced in fictive carving as part of the architectural settings of the three panels, bringing a wealth of scriptural references to the work. The humanity, the accessibility of Christ and his mother, affectivity too, are the very basis also of the pair of panels showing the *Virgin Fainting* and *Christ on the Cross* (Johnson Collection, Philadelphia).

With these visual texts in our minds, if we look at the times in which Roger van der Weyden lived, we find that he has translated into visual terms the essence of a spiritual movement which was at the peak of its development during his lifetime – the *Devotio Moderna*. Reading the pages on the *Devotio Moderna* written by Dom François Vandenbroucke,[23] we find phrases like these: 'affective piety', 'an intense spiritual life', 'intensity of love', 'a call to conversion, meditation, imitation of the life and death of Christ', 'the imitation of the manhood of Christ'. The most famous writer to come from this movement was undoubtedly Thomas à Kempis, and even today his *Imitation of Christ* is still widely read. Thomas à Kempis had a long life, living into his nineties. His date bracket: 1379/80-1471, is of particular interest here because it embraces that of Roger van der Weyden: 1399/1400-1464. The basic tendencies of the writings of Thomas à Kempis, again to quote Vandenbroucke, are 'affective devotion and contemplation of Christ's humanity'.[24] 'In the Imitation', writes Vandenbroucke, 'we find summed up the principal tendencies of spirituality in the first half of the fifteenth century'.[25]

2 Fra Angelico, *Annunciation*, Prado, Madrid

Clearly, we can make a similar claim for the paintings of Roger van der Weyden.

When we look at the work of Roger's contemporary and fellow-artist, the Dominican Friar, Fra Giovanni da Fiesole, Blessed Angelico,we are conscious of entering a different world. The *Annunciation* altarpiece in the Prado, Madrid, comes from a chapel in the public church attached to the friary of San Domenico at Fiesole, where Fra Giovanni was a member of the community. An atmosphere of serenity pervades the scene. Mary's attitude conveys her spirit of acceptance, obedience, humility. She fully understands, accepts and agrees to the message which the archangel Gabriel brings. There is no hesitation here, no doubt, no fear. Mary believes. We want to cry out: 'Blessed is she who believed.' This is an image of faith.

There is also a subsidiary scene in this altarpiece, the scene of the expulsion of Adam and Eve from the garden of paradise. Adam and Eve look guilt-ridden as they are driven out by the angel. Their very attitude, their body-language, conveys a message of punishment, dismissal, loss. We are being reminded that because of their disobedience, mankind fell from grace. But now, as we read in the main scene, there is a new Eve – Mary – and through her obedience, she becomes at this moment the mother of the new Adam – Christ the Saviour, sent to redeem us.

In this altarpiece, therefore, Fra Angelico is appealing, not to the emotions, but to the intellect. He invites us to reflect upon this mystery, not only in the sense of imagining to ourselves what the scene and the setting might have looked like, but in theological terms.

What Saint Dominic most wanted to do was the work of preaching. His new Order was to have 'the title and function of Preacher'[26] – the Order of Preachers. Its concerns were, from the beginning, preaching, study and the practice of evangelical poverty, in order to teach the rule of faith and win souls for Christ.[27] Its mission was doctrinal and apostolic. Set up in a public place, the altarpiece now in the Prado is, therefore, a perfect expression of that mission. Doctrinally exact, it conveys the message, that is, it preaches faith and obedience to the will of God.

When we turn to the paintings made by Fra Angelico in the friary of San Marco in Florence, we come even closer to the heart of Dominican spirituality, because what Angelico painted there, in the friary itself, as distinct from the public church attached to it, was intended solely for the friars themselves, and not for the general public. Indeed, the public would not normally be there at all. At the end of one side of the cloister, Angelico painted a *Crucified Christ* with St Dominic kneeling at the foot of the cross (fig. 4). This is not an historical representation of the Crucifixion scene, nor is it particularly pathetic. It does not evoke an emotional response. It does, however, demand of the spectator standing in front of it an identification with St Dominic, whose gaze meets Christ's as he hangs on the cross. In the conversation which passes between them, Dominic loses himself in contemplation. Afterwards, he will bring the fruits of his contemplation to others, in his preaching. This is an image of that Dominican ideal: *Contemplare, et contemplata aliis tradere*, to contemplate, and to pass on to others the fruits of contemplation.

Facing the top of the stairs which lead to the upper corridor, is another *Annunciation* scene. The figures of Mary and the angel appear as they do in the Prado altarpiece, but the scene of Adam and Eve is omitted. This version is not an aid to preaching, but nourishment for the prayer of the friar who would fix his gaze on it as he mounted the stairs

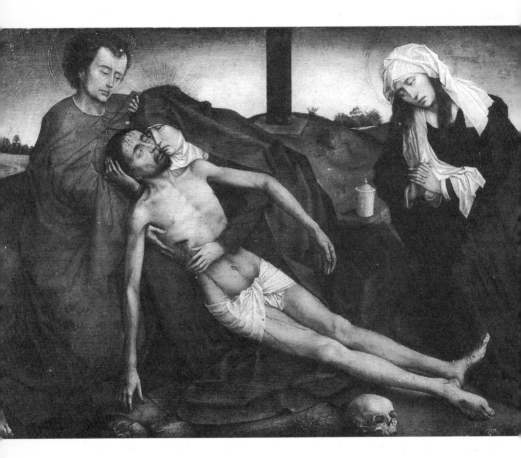

3 Roger van der Weyden, *Pietà*, or Lamentation over the Body of Christ,
Musées Royaux des Beaux-Arts de Belgique, Brussels

to his cell. As he drew close, he could read the words inscribed on it: 'Hail Mother of devotion and dwelling-place of the entire Trinity'.[28] As he passed by, he would notice another inscription reminding him not to neglect to say an Ave in front of this image of the immaculate Virgin.[29] Then, in his cell, he would have constantly before his eyes another sacred scene painted by Fra Angelico, always with the figures of Mary and St Dominic present in it, in the same spirit as in the Crucifixion in the cloister corridor.

This art, created by the Dominican painter for his Dominican brethren, has as its purpose to be a stepping-stone to prayer, meditation, communion with God. But it also in itself expresses that very spirituality which it is intended to assist. It possesses the contemplative and intellectual qualities of the Dominican way. Indeed, it is fascinating to put beside these visual images, the words of a Dominican preacher, a Florentine who lived about one hundred years earlier than Fra Angelico – Fra Jacopo Passavanti (*c.*1302-57). In the introduction to his book entitled *Specchio di vera penitenzia* (1354), Passavanti sets out the order, the structure of his essay. He does so 'because orderliness, precision, openness and clarity lead to insight'.[30] Orderliness, precision, openness and clarity – surely these are also among the qualities of Angelico's work. They are qualities useful to the preacher who uses painted images, as well as to the preacher who uses the spoken or the written word.

Clearly, the comparisons and studies which form the basis of this essay are but a small indication of the wealth of images into which ideas concerning the spiritual life have been translated, in the Christian tradition. From them more than one conclusion may be drawn, but that which it seems most urgent to proclaim is, that, as we respect and celebrate the various facets and styles of Christian spirituality as genuine expressions of the movement of the Holy Spirit, so must we respect and have regard for the richly varied works of art which reflect those various facets and styles. There is no one, single, 'correct' style of art in the service of spirituality, either now, in this present age, or in the past. In the words of Pope John Paul II, spoken on the occasion of a visit to the shrine of our Lady of Jasna Gora, in Poland: 'The image of Jasna Gora is a great work of art. Divine Providence makes use of the work of human hands, of works of art and human genius, in order to bring the truth closer to our minds and hearts. God works through man's works of art. Man's work becomes, as it were, a visible sign of the Divine Mystery.'

4 Fra Angelico, *St Dominic at the Foot of the Cross*, San Marco, Florence

NOTES

1 See Jean Leclercq, *Bernard of Clairvaux and the Cistercian Spirit* (Kalamazoo, 1976), pp. 51ff.
2 The text is given in full, trans. by Michael Casey OCSO, with an intro. by Jean Leclercq OSB, in *The Works of Bernard of Clairvaux*, i, Treatises 1, Cistercian Fathers Series (Shannon, 1970), pp. 33-69.
3 For the context of the Apologia, in the atmosphere of 'jealous rivalry' between the Cistercian and Cluniac observances, see Ailbe J. Luddy, O.Cist, *Life and Teaching of St Bernard* (Dublin, 1927), pp. 94ff.
4 Treatises 1 (as n.2), p. 52.
5 Treatises 1 (as n.2), p. 48.
6 Treatises 1 (as n.2), p. 63-6.
7 The ground-plan of Cluny III, drawn up by Professor Conant, is reproduced in R. Oursel, *Bourgogne Romane* (La-Pierre-qui-Vire, 1974), p. 100.
8 R. Oursel, op. cit., p. 140.
9 It is possible that some, at least, of the capitals were already carved before the fire of 1120. See: R. Oursel, op. cit., p. 284.
10 Pontigny, the second daughter-house of Cîteaux, was founded in 1114, and its church was still building, at the time of Bernard's death, in 1153.
11 *Abbot Suger on the Abbey Church of St-Denis and its Art Treasures* edited, translated and annotated by Erwin Panofsky (Princeton, 1946), pp 65-7.
12 Suger also wrote the biographies of the two kings he served.
13 On Saint-Denis, see also Alain Erlande-Brandebourg, *La Basilique Saint-Denis* (Rennes, 1981).
14 *Abbot Suger* ... as n. 11, pp. 47-9.
15 Ibid., p.101.
16 Ibid., p. 75.
17 Suger is here referring to Ezek 28:13. See also the description of Aaron's 'pectoral of judgement' in Ex 28:17-20.
18 *Abbot Suger* ... as n. 11, pp. 63-5.
19 For Bernard's side of the correspondence between him and Suger see *The Letters of St Bernard of Clairvaux*, trans. by Bruno Scott James (London, 1953).
20 Fra Giovanni da Fiesole, long since known in Italy as Beato Angelico was declared Blessed by the present Holy Father, Pope John Paul II. In the case of Roger van der Weyden, it is evident both from surviving documents concerning him and from his paintings that he led a devoutly Christian life. See Odile Delenda, *Rogier van der Weyden* (Paris, 1987), passim.
21 The painting is on wood and measures 220 cm in height by 262 cm in width.
22 This painting is also on wood. It is much smaller than the Madrid painting. It measures 32 cm h. by 48 cm w.
23 In Jean Leclercq et al., *A History of Christian Spirituality*, ii, *The Spirituality of the Middle Ages* (London, 1968), pp. 428-39.

24 Ibid., p. 437.

25 Ibid., p. 438.

26 Ibid., p. 316, quoting Vicaire, *Histoire de saint Dominique,* ii, p. 17.

27 On Dominican spirituality, see Vandenbroucke, op. cit., p. 315 ff.

28 *Salve Mater Pietatis et totius Trinitatis triclinium.* The translation given here is, it need hardly be said, approximate.

29 *Virginis intacte cum veneris ante figuram, praetereundo cave ne sileatur Ave.*

30 Daniel R. Lesnick, *Preaching in Medieval Florence. The social world of Franciscan and Dominican spirituality* (Athens [Georgia] and London, 1989), p. 101.

Imaging God: Spiritual Dimensions in Modern Art

GESA THIESSEN

THE WORK OF ART AS A SOURCE OF REVELATION

In 1880 Vincent van Gogh wrote to his brother Theo:

> I think that everything that is really good and beautiful, of inner moral, spiritual and sublime beauty in [humans] ... and their works, comes from God, and that all that is bad and wrong in [humans] ... and in their works is not of God, and God does not approve of it. But I always think that the best way to know God is to love many things ... To give you an example: someone loves Rembrandt ... that [person] ... will know that there is a God, he [she] will surely believe it ... To try to understand the real significance of what the great artists, the serious masters, tell us in their masterpieces, *that* leads to God.'[1]

Van Gogh conveys something in these lines which is of fundamental importance to all human existence, and in particular to how the human relates to and comes to know the divine. It is the simple statement that in order to know God one must love. It is, as he says, through the love of many things, and of people for that matter, that one learns about and deepens one's knowledge of God. Loving many things and thus knowing God means for van Gogh the love of all that is good, truthful and beautiful, and so, speaking out of his own experience, he insists that the great masterpieces make one see that God – who is Him/Herself supreme beauty, truth and goodness – exists, that they make us believe.

This then is the point of departure for my essay. It is in line with the overall aim of this book which is to explore and show that the transcendent is indeed not merely to be perceived and experienced in Sunday worship, in the sacraments or in church doctrines, but rather that one can get glimpses of the divine in other, and so called more secular, spheres of life also, such as through the love and appreciation of music, poetry and visual art. It is through one's openess to an encounter

97

with art that we may unexpectedly feel, taste, hear or see what Paul Tillich describes as 'ultimate reality'.[2]

While traditional theology has had little room for mystical, sensuous and non-conceptual experiences of the divine, it is perhaps a sign of the times that the need for an integration of the arts into a wider theological agenda has been increasingly recognised in recent years. As Frank Burch Brown has observed, traditional theological discourse strives to be 'logically consistent, coherent, comprehensive, conceptually precise' whereas art does not seek doctrinal clarity and precise concepts but rather reveals 'fictively, metaphorically, and experientially what formal theology cannot itself present or contain'.[3]

In being aware that the divine and our faith are far greater realities than theological concepts and doctrines manage to express, theologians and other scholars such as Tillich, von Balthasar and Rahner, and in more recent times, Diane Apostolos-Cappadona, John and Jane Dillenberger, Richard Harries, George Pattison, Horst Schwebel and Guenter Rombold and others have made pleas and concrete attempts of integrating (visual) art, into theological studies.[4] These theologians work on the basis that the work of art, that is, the visual image, *like* the written word, is and must be treated as a *primary* document of human expression. In regarding the image as equal to and not something lesser than the word, these scholars, of both Protestant and Roman Catholic backgrounds, would therefore emphasise that the work of art can have a truly revelatory effect and dimension. Here it is particularly important to keep in mind that the contemporary discussion on the relationship of faith and art does not focus on modern church art, but rather on the spiritual in modern art as such. What is being explored is a much broader concept of what can be described as the spiritual or religious in twentieth century art.[5]

The particular and often awkward task then of developing a theology of (modern) art, i.e. a theology based on the material image rather than on the written word, is to try to articulate what ultimately is beyond words, namely the transcendent and religious dimensions in a work of art. This attempt to describe what lies beyond words, as well as the plurality of interpretations is *the* challenge on which a theology of and through art is based. Paradoxically perhaps, it is this somewhat fragile point of departure which gives this theology its ultimate strength, life and *raison d'être*.[6]

1 Georges Rouault, *Ecce Homo* (1938–9)

FROM PASSION TO SALVATION – RELIGIOUS AND
SPIRITUAL ASPECTS IN SIX TWENTIETH-CENTURY
WORKS OF ART

Georges Rouault, Ecce Homo *(1938-9)*

Georges Rouault (1871-1958) has been described as a truly modern religious artist.[7] In his work he concerned himself primarily with the dark
side of human existence, its fears and suffering. A devout Catholic[8]
Rouault wished to be able some day to paint Christ in such a moving
manner that those who would see the image would be converted.

The forms, techniques and the spirit of his works are expressionist in
style.[9] Throughout his life Rouault's subject matter was strongly religious; it includes many images of Christ's passion which often are reminiscent of icons as well as of stained glass art.[10]

When one looks at *Ecce Homo* – a Christ who has calmly resigned
himself to his fate – one is reminded of what Rouault once wrote about
himself: 'I am the silent friend of all those who labour in the fields, I am
the ivy of eternal wretchedness clinging to the leprous wall behind
which rebellious humanity hides its vices and its virtues alike', and he
added 'Being a Christian in these hazardous times, I can only believe in
Christ on the cross'.[11] It is interesting to note that Rouault speaks here
as if he himself was Christ. Among twentieth-century artists he was not
the only one to identify with Christ, a fact which reflects the isolated
position of the modern artist in society, especially in the earlier part of
this century.[12]

Ecce Homo then is both expressive and still. It provokes sympathy in
the viewer and invites contemplation. Although both the title and the
depiction clearly emphasise Christ's suffering, the sun in the background
as well as the golden dabs of colour on the horizon and around Christ's
head, the hint of a halo, indicate his divinity and the anticipation of the
resurrection and salvation. This painting is therefore an example of how
eschatological hope, resurrection and glory are conveyed in modern art.
Rather than direct images, it is predominantly only bright colour and
light which indicate or symbolise the soteriological dimension and eternal life. This clearly reflects the predicament of the twentieth century
where secularisation and the horrors of the two world wars, injustice,
and hunger have made a simple, unquestioning trust and faith in a life
thereafter impossible. Salvific hope is therefore hinted at rather than
explicitly stated in modern art.

2 Pablo Picasso, *Guernica* (1937)

Pablo Picasso, Guernica *(1937)*

Pablo Picasso (1881-1973) painted *Guernica*, one of his masterpieces, in 1937 on the occasion of the bombardment and complete destruction of the village Guernica by Franco in the Spanish Civil War.[13] The viewer is presented with a scene of utter horror, a woman who kneels over her dead child, the bull a symbol of brutality, the wounded horse a symbol of humanity, the wounded soldier with outstretched arms reminiscent of the crucifixion, as well as the woman seemingly locked into a cell with her arms thrown upwards in a silent cry, and a figure who looks through the window and holds up a candle which illumes the scene. This figure is the viewer, speechless in the face of such horror.

Guernica is an expression of Picasso's outrage at the atrocities of Fascism and war. He maintained that his works were never deliberately propagandist[14] but with regard to *Guernica* he stated in 1945: 'Only the *Guernica* mural is symbolic ... That's the reason I've used the horse, the bull, and so on ... In that there is a deliberate appeal to the people, a deliberate sense of propaganda ...'[15]

Guernica in its depiction of the horrors of war and violence is a deeply existentialist painting. In its appeal to humankind to come to its senses, in its portrayal of innocent human suffering and in its pictorial allusions to the crucified, this awe-inspiring work can *in some sense* be described as a modern crucifixion.[16]

Barnett Newman, 'Lema Sabachthani', The Stations of the Cross *(1958-66)*

The American Jewish painter Barnett Newman belongs to the generation of the Abstract Expressionists, together with Rothko, Motherwell, de Kooning, Pollock and others, who emerged around 1950. Individuality, non-conformity, an emphasis on painting as a way of life, and stress on the act of painting as an expression of 'authentic being', rather than on the finished product distinguishes these artists.[17]

Newman painted a number of works which were biblically inspired, such as *Covenant, The Beginning, Day One* and *Lema Sabachthani.*[18] There are no recognisable forms in the fourteen canvases of the *Stations,* except for the black and white lines and spaces. However, the impact of black and white alters from canvas to canvas. First, white is dominant, then there are increasingly black areas, black dominates in the twelfth and thirteenth station while in the fourteenth white finally triumphs.

Why did Newman paint these works? He said that they portrayed his understanding of the Passion and that he tried to evoke the 'lema', the 'why' of the crucifixion.[19] Newman is thus concerned with the incarnate God who suffers for the redemption of humankind. At the same time he asks the ultimate question *why* God needs to suffer.

Newman wrote that for him art is not just personal expression, but an exploration of the metaphysical dimensions of the secret of the world. In this way, he states, art becomes religious as it tries to perceive through symbols the fundamental truth of life.[20]

It is significant that and how Newman depicts the crucifixion without any figurative images. Apart from the fact that his interest was in abstract art, another, perhaps unconscious, reason for his non-figurative approach in this and other works with religious allusions, may have been his Jewish background with its iconoclastic emphasis.

Newman thus provides us with an image of God which fuses Old Testament theology of the impossibility and prohibition of material images of the divine with Pauline christology which explicitly refers to Christ as the *eikon* of the invisible God which in turn is the basis for the possibility of images (not idols!) of God (cf. 2 Cor 4: 4; Rom 8: 29-30). In these *Stations of the Cross* God is acknowledged as incarnate and immanent, while at the same time, because of the absence of any figuration, S/He remains the totally other, total mystery, the God who is always greater and ultimately beyond words or paint. *Lema Sabachthani* therefore reveals God's humanity and divinity, immanence and transcendence, suffering and glory.

3 Barnett Newman, *Station #13* (1965/66)

It is quite remarkable, and perhaps significant, that it was a Jew rather than an artist of Christian background, who would find such an economic, yet striking, visual language to convey the central Christian paradox, that is, God who is both human and divine, which constitutes the ground of our trinitarian faith.

Harry Clarke, The Angel of Peace and Hope *(1919)*

This stained glass window was designed by Harry Clarke (1889-1931) for the Holy Trinity Church in Killiney, Dublin. Clarke, with Evie Hone the foremost Irish stained glass artist of this century, received the commission from a Mrs Lloyd in memory of her young son who had been killed during the First World War.[21]

In Clarke's work several stylistic elements find expression. Greatly influenced by Beardsley, a celtic revivalist like William Butler Yeats and George Russell (AE), Clarke's art can be described in terms of symbolism, national romanticism, celtic mysticism, decadence and *art nouveau.*[22]

The Angel of Peace and Hope, especially the face and hands, strongly resemble figures by Beardsley.[23] The flowing red hair conveys something of the celtic-romantic, the clothes are highly decorative and reveal intricate details of flowers. The dove is a Christian symbol of peace, the halo, staff and wings are symbolic of angels.

However, if one thinks of traditional depictions of angels, as in Renaissance art, for example, this one is clearly different. Except for the symbols this figure appears strangely human, more female than male, with an aura of the fantastic and of temptation.

It is interesting to note that despite the Church's rather ambivalent, if not negative, attitude towards the body and the sensual, many of Clarke's works made their way into churches all over Ireland. This probably happened because he rightly became recognised as an outstanding artist who displayed an amazing vision, power and skill.

James White, in his foreword to Nicola Gordon Bowe's book on Clarke, emphasises that all great art is based on conflict and that in Clarke's work the sensual-mystical tension is particularly apparent.[24] Clarke never was a devout Catholic[25] and in his art he created ecstatically beautiful, yet decadent and disturbing images which testify to this lifelong conflict in the artist. *The Angel of Peace and Hope* serves as a striking example of this tension in his work.

Clarke's son Michael wrote in 1988 about the influence of religion in his father's life: 'Much of religion in which he did not believe he found aesthetically pleasing. The peripheral rules he found an irritation. The deeper mysteries filled him with awe.'[26]

4 The Angel of Peace and Hope (detail; 1919)

F.E. McWilliam, Princess Macha *(1957)*

McWilliam, a prolific sculptor from the North of Ireland, has been described as the 'foremost Irish sculptor of his generation' and, since he spent many years in England, as one of the best artists in the isles.[27] In his works he concentrated primarily on the human figure. Stylistically McWilliam was an eclectic. Influences by Picasso and Giacometti are apparent in several of his works.

In the *Princess Macha* sculpture in bronze, one of the most important commissions in the artist's career, Giacometti's influence is particularly apparent in the elongated and very thin figure.[28]

Queen Macha is a goddess in celtic mythology. Different stories are attached to her; as the wife of Nemed she is described as a visionary, another story shows her as the dominant wife of Cumbaeth whose lands she acquires, and in a third story she is the divine bride of Crunn to whom she brings prosperity but Crunn then betrays her. Thus Macha can be seen in terms of visionary, warrior and bestower of wealth and fertility. Basically the word Macha means 'plain' or 'field', as well as 'crow' or 'blackbird'. Macha is connected with Ulster; interestingly and ironically Ard Macha or Armagh, the pagan high place became the seat of Christian primacy in Ireland.[29]

What is striking and relevant about McWilliam's sculpture is its mixture of pagan-celtic and christian elements.[30] The figure, seated with outstretched, welcoming arms, the crow replaced by a dove, the calm oval face are reminiscent of Byzantine and late medieval depictions of the Virgin. The surface is crinkled and pocked. It vaguely evokes the intricate details one finds in celtic art, such as in the Book of Kells.

Princess Macha is thus a good example of what McWilliam as well as other Irish artists have revealed in their work – the fusion of pagan-celtic myths, themes and art with Christian subject matter.[31]

McWilliam once said:

> Mystery is terribly important, in art as in religion. I mean if you take the mystery out of religion you're only left with morality, and if you take the mystery out of art you're only left with design or illustration ... What it does is to give you just that difference from everyday reality ... The trick is not to go away from this world but to make something just a little bit different. That's where the mystery comes in.[32]

5 F.E. McWilliam, *Princess Macha* (1957)

Patrick Scott, Chinese Landscape J '86 *(1986)*

Born in 1921 Patrick Scott is renowned nationally and internationally as an abstract artist. The critic Dorothy Walker has said that the 'essence of Patrick Scott's work lies in his own exquisite aesthetic sensibility'.[33]

Predominantly without subject matter, Scott's works display a sense for the formal, geometrical and linear.[34] Interestingly in several of his works Scott applies media which were used in Early Renaissance art, such as gold leaf and tempera, on raw canvas.[35]

The sun (in gold leaf) is a repeated feature in his paintings. The sun as symbol can be traced back into Antiquity and was adopted into Christian art where it is used as an attribute of the allegorical figure of Truth as all is revealed by its light and all revelation brings light.[36] The sun also features in Celtic art and this together with Scott's interest in geometric, abstract forms as well as in circular shapes makes a link with Ireland's celtic past.[37]

Moreover, Scott has an interest in the Far East which the title of the present painting indicates. Eastern Buddhist spirituality and Zen art has, in fact, influenced a number of modern artists in the West, notably some of the nineteenth-century Impressionists and Post-Impressionists and later individual painters like Mark Tobey, for example.

In *Chinese Landscape J '86* the sharply defined semi-circle of the sun contrasts with a highly simplified landscape of mountains. Some of the peaks recede into the background and seem to merge with the sky. The overall mood in this as in other paintings by the artist is that of calm and stillness. In its stylised depiction, its simple grandeur and meditative aspect, this Chinese landscape acquires a universal, cosmic dimension which through its almost ephemeral atmosphere conveys a sense of the sublime and of transcendence. The sun towers over this Chinese land-scape and therefore over the whole earth and by its power draws all nature and being towards its eternal light.

CONCLUSION

Traditionally the religious and/or the spiritual in art in the West has been equated with the art of the medieval period, the Renaissance and the Baroque, i.e. with that art which displays explicit Christian subject matter. The intention in this essay has been to show, that we do, in fact, find significant and far-ranging transcendent and even explicitly religious (christian) dimensions in twentieth century art also, even if they are

6 Patrick Scott, *Chinese Landscape J '86* (1986)

indirect, individualistic, enigmatic or provocative, rather than clear and doctrinal as in older art.

The six works of art shown here give a small glimpse of the variety of spiritual aspects in modern art: the christocentric approach in Rouault, the political-existentialist thrust in Picasso's *Guernica*, the christological, eschatological and transcendent dimension in Newman's work, the fusion of pagan-celtic and christian elements in McWilliam, the decadent-sublime religious aspect in Clarke, and finally the eastern/universal transcendent dimension in Scott.

There are many other (post)modern artists whose work reveals explicit or implicit religious and spiritual aspects such as the ecstatic and visionary paintings by the Expressionist painter Nolde, the surrealist-religious works by Dali, the strongly expressionist-christological paintings by Corinth, the mythological-christian subjects in Beuys, and the abstract-transcendent works by artists like Kandinsky, Rothko, Ad Reinhardt and Agnes Martin.[38] These are only a few artists among those whose works still need to be explored in much more detail from a theological point of view.

The theological and spiritual dimensions in twentieth-century art reveal something of the breath of human existence and religious experience: life and death, immanence and transcendence, suffering and redemption, creation and salvation, faith, doubt, anti-ecclesiastical tendencies and, on a few occasions, explicit atheism. With regard to religious subject matter the figure of Christ, as the one who suffers for and with humankind, plays a predominant role in many contemporary works. This reflects the situation of our century where humans have experienced and, through the media, are much more aware of suffering than in any previous epoch.

Imaging God in modern art is far removed from the dogmatic works of the Counter-Reformation with their task of educating the illiterate faithful in matters of Christian faith. The spiritual in contemporary art is not easily grasped, because we ourselves, the artist included, do not easily believe in an age, which is secular and humanist rather than theocentric.

The contemporary artist creates works which are essentially born of individual vision and personal experience. What we *can* learn from the art of today, however, is the fact that the spiritual, in whatever unusual, enigmatic or even outrageous form, continues to be revealed in modern works; that faith in Christ (implicitly or explicitly) or at least in the transcendent continues to play a significant role in the lives and works of many artists. In fact, one may suggest that all great art is spiritual because it is essentially born of the spirit, i.e. of what is most profound in the individual human soul, mind and experience.

The sculptor Henry Moore once said:

> Artists, in a way, are religious anyway. They have to be; if by religion one means believing that life has some significance, and some meaning, which is what I think it has. An artist could not work without believing that.[39]

This points us to the fundamental link between religion and art, the theologian and the artist. It is the question and exploration in words or in paint of what concerns the human person at the deepest level, i.e. one's existence in the world which includes the ultimate quest for meaning and for the divine. The artist as God's co-creator, the work of art as revelation of truth, goodness and beauty, the possibility of verbal and pictorial images of the sacred, which, of course, are never more than glimpses of the unfathomable divine, these aspects are at the heart of religion, art and theology.

Finally, I would argue, that precisely because of the lack of dogmatic certainties in modern works of art, because interpretations therefore must remain open rather than definite, because the works are often more mysterious than clear in their message, they can truly enrich, challenge and broaden contemporary theology and the spiritual life of the church and of each individual who is prepared to see in new ways.

NOTES

1 Mark Roskill (ed.), *The Letters of Vincent van Gogh* (London, 1983), pp. 123-4.

2 See Paul Tillich, 'Art and Ultimate Reality' (1960), in *Paul Tillich – Main Works*, ed. Michael Palmer, ii (Berlin and New York, 1990), pp. 317-32. Tillich writes: 'The term "ultimate reality" is *not* another name for God in the religious sense of the word. But the God of religion would not be God if he were not first of all ultimate reality' (p. 318). Tillich was, in fact, one of the first theologians to write on the spiritual and religious aspects in modern art. According to him there are three ways through which humans express and experience ultimate reality, metaphysics and art being the indirect path, religion being the direct way.

3 Frank Burch Brown, *Religious Aesthetics* (Princeton, 1989), pp. 166-7.

4 For an introduction into the whole area of theology and art see, for example, Diane Apostolos-Cappadona (ed.), *Art, Creativity and the Sacred, An Anthology in Religion and Art* (New York, 1988).

5 See the introduction in Wendy Beckett, *Art and the Sacred* (London, 1992),

where Beckett discusses the meaning of and differentiates between the 'religious', the 'spiritual', and the 'sacred' in art. Whereas religious art shows explicit religious subject matter, spiritual art, she writes, can only be known through its 'personal power' (p. 10).

6 The hermeneutical problem in art is essentially the same as in texts. Like a text a work of art will be interpreted differently by different (theological) scholars. In our postmodern age claims for one authoritative interpretation of a work of art can no longer be made. Naturally this implies 'danger' of too much subjectivity on the one hand, but also, on the other hand, the possibility of a rich variety of interpretations which may arrive at greater truth than those interpretations which claim exclusive authority. On the hermeneutical problem see Werner G. Jeanrond, *Theological Hermeneutics: Development and Significance* (London, 1991), esp. ch. 7, and Anne Sheppard, *Aesthetics* (Oxford, 1987), esp, ch. 6

7 See Jane Dillenberger, *Style and Content in Christian Art* (London, 1965), p. 206.

8 James Thrall Soby, *Georges Rouault – Paintings and Prints* (New York, 1945[?]), p. 5.

9 Peter and Linda Murray, *Dictionary of Art and Artists* (London, 1989), p. 367.

10 Rouault had in fact been trained in stained glass art; see Guenter Rombold, *Der Streit um das Bild – Zum Verhaeltnis von moderner Kunst und Religion* (Stuttgart, 1988), p. 158.

11 See Guenter Rombold and Horst Schwebel, *Christus in der Kunst des 20. Jahrhunderts* (Basel and Wien, 1983), p. 43.

12 Gauguin, for example, portrayed himself in several of his paintings as a Christ figure.

13 See Herbert Read, *A Concise History of Modern Painting* (London, 1974), pp. 160-2.

14 Herschel B. Chipp, *Theories of Modern Art* (Berkeley and Los Angeles, 1968), p. 489.

15 Excerpt from an interview with Pfc. Jerome Seckler, 'Picasso Explains', *New Masses* (New York, LIV, II, 13 March 1945), pp. 4-7, in Chipp (as n.14), pp. 487, 489.

16 Of course, one can interpret this work only *in some sense* as a crucifixion as the figure of Christ on the cross is not actually present but only alluded to.

17 Harold Osborne, *The Oxford Companion to Art* (Oxford, 1970), pp. 3-4. Because of the emphasis on the physical act of painting abstract expressionism is also termed 'action painting'.

18 Rombold (as n. 10), p. 133.

19 Rombold (as n. 10), p. 137.

20 Maurice Tuchman (ed.), *The Spiritual in Art: Abstract Painting 1890-1985* (New York, 1986), p. 49 quoted (in German translation) in Rombold (as n. 10), p. 138.

21 Nicola Gordon Bowe, *Harry Clarke* (exhibition catalogue) (Dublin, 1979), p. 104.

22 Nicola Gordon Bowe, *The Life and Work of Harry Clarke* (Dublin, 1989), pp. 1-3.

23 Clarke actually referred to the window as the 'Beardsley window'; see Bowe (as n. 21), p. 104.

24 James White, foreword in N.G. Bowe (as n. 22), p. xiv.

25 Michael Clarke's statement about his father, quoted by J. White in his foreword in N.G. Bowe, (as n. 22), p. xiii.

26 Michael Clarke (as n. 25), p. xiii.

27 Brian Fallon wrote this on the occasion of the sculptor's death in 1992, *Irish Times*, 14 September 1992.

28 Judy Marle and T.P. Flanagan, *F.E. McWilliam* (Belfast and Dublin, [1981]), p. 17.

29 I thank John de Paor for the information on the story of Princess Macha.

30 Marle and Flanagan (as n. 28), p. 24.

31 Gerard Dillon and Jack Yeats in some of their works, for example.

32 Marle and Flanagan (as n. 28), p. 17.

33 Article by Dorothy Walker on Scott, in *Patrick Scott* (exhibition cat.) (Dublin, 1981), p. 15.

34 Walker (as n. 33), pp. 15, 26.

35 Elizabeth Mayes and Paula Murphy (eds.), *Images and Insights* (Dublin, 1993), p. 136.

36 James Hall, *Dictionary of Subjects and Symbols in Art* (London, 1984), p. 292.

37 Mayes and Murphy, (as n. 35).

38 For more literature on the spiritual in modern art see the writings by Dillenberger, Kandinsky's *Concerning the Spiritual in Art* (orig. publ. in German in 1911), Guenter Rombold and Horst Schwebel (only available in German), Doug Adams, John Dillenberger.

39 R. Harries, *Art and the Beauty of God* (London, 1993), pre ch. 1 (no pagination).

Witnesses and Prophets: Some Soundings in Recent Irish Writings

JOHN DEVITT

The sheer rapidity with which Irish society has changed during the past twenty years or so is a cause of wonder though it has also generated considerable anxiety, especially among those who have passed the meridian of their lives. Familiar landmarks have disappeared; authorities of all kinds have lost face and are seized by unfamiliar doubts; the life-styles adopted by children astonish and dismay their parents; men and women of good will are bewildered as vistas of increasing uncertainty open up before them. We seem to live in a moral and metaphysical hiatus 'between two worlds, one dead,/ The other powerless to be born', to quote Mathew Arnold's irresistible lines. The old certainties have a dilapidated appearance and there is a distinctly uncomfortable sense abroad that they cannot be restored and may never be replaced. Not surprisingly, futile reaction, driven by nostalgia for an irretrievable past which may never have existed, has gathered many new recruits, but cynicism and despair are inevitable subscribers to every reactionary movement.

Yet this same period has been astonishingly fruitful in the arts. It is no exaggeration to say that we have witnessed a literary revival as remarkable in the range and scope of its achievements as the one inaugurated by Yeats at the end of the last century. A future historian, with all the confidence of hindsight, will clarify the connections between the fluid condition of society in our time and the masterworks of writers, North and South, in all the established literary forms. Such insights are not available to us. Rather than speculate fancifully about such imponderable questions, I propose to engage in the patient and detailed analysis of a handful of very recent texts which have a special claim on our attention. One cannot articulate 'the meanings' of any literary work without experiencing it as intimately as the limitations of one's sensibility permits; that means respecting its form, registering its internal dynamics and relishing its verbal texture. It is, of course, no part of my intention to suggest that literature, much less literary criticism, can save us, though I would argue that a society's attempts at self-understanding could hardly find a more promising place to begin. Poems, plays and novels of real imaginative intensity witness to things as they are and often speak in a genuinely prophetic idiom. Not that the spiritual quotient of imaginative literature is generally welcomed or even recognised. In the course of his 1995 Ernest Jones Lecture, the poet James Fenton remarked: 'That the fight between art and religion is an ancient and a necessary one we may concede, since all art tends to arrogate authority to itself, and all religion aspires to a monopoly on authority.'[1] The quarrel is certainly an old one, but it may not be necessary; a church, instructed by experience and the voices of imagination, is not inconceivable.[2]

II

> From the conservative dark
> Into the ethical life
> The dense commuters come ...

I have chosen these lines from W.H. Auden's great poem '1 September 1939' as an epigraph to this section because they indicate the nature of the difference imaginative literature makes to those who receive it freely. Auden did not suppose that his poem would change the course of history or that it would supply a solution to the problem presented by the German invasion of Poland. He did not presume that poetry could do the work of politics without ceasing to be poetry. In fact, in his virtually contemporaneous elegy on the death of W.B. Yeats he insisted that 'poetry makes nothing happen' before going on to show in beautifully chiselled rhyming couplets that its real importance lies elsewhere, in its capacity to educate the feelings and the spirit.

> With the farming of this verse
> Make a vineyard of the curse,
> Sing of human unsuccess
> In a rapture of distress;
> In the deserts of the heart,
> Let the healing fountain start
> In the prison of his days
> Teach the free man how to praise.[3]

Auden achieves high seriousness while remaining intensely and gravely playful; the pleasure he communicates through the rhymes and images and especially through the rhythmical intricacies of the verse are finally inseparable from the almost prayerful posture he adopts.

Poetry helps to make us more human, more alive as spiritual and sentient beings and it does this through processes which are pleasurable and delightful. Even when it dramatises and celebrates a morality issuing splendidly in action, the poetic effect is irreducible. There is an unforgettable moment of great spiritual and emotional clarity in Virgil's *Aeneid* which I want to recall. After the long siege Troy finally falls to the Greeks; its towers are engulfed in flames; its inhabitants are ruthlessly and indiscriminately put to the sword. A pitiful remnant of the Trojans under the leadership of Aeneas prepares to flee the stricken city. Conscious that he himself is polluted by the blood he has shed and is therefore unworthy to handle sacred objects, Aeneas entrusts the household gods of Troy to his father Anchises before stooping to take the enfeebled old man on his shoulders; his own son Iulus grasps his right hand while his wife Creusa follows close behind. This is the very image of *pietas* (piety) in its old pre-Christian sense. Aeneas' actions testify to his loyalty to the sources of his being, both human and divine; but he is simultaneously concerned for the future as represented by his son and agitated by the plight of his wife. You might feel disposed to argue that this rich Virgilian *pietas* is a virtue which is needful in our time, as always, and you might wonder why we have lost sight of it. But before we abandon ourselves to the ethical discourse the passage invites, we might attend for a moment to its poetic power. Virgil makes us see, hear and smell the doomed city; he makes us one with the bewildered refugees; he enlists our imagination. One detail will have to suffice. Iulus, we are told, follows his father with '*non passibus aequis*', literally 'with unequal steps'.[4] In the middle of this scene of terrible desolation and exquisite 'piety', we see the young boy trotting absurdly beside his father; we have, indeed, no choice but to see. In this instance poetic power is entirely and miraculously consonant with enormous pathos.

Christianity has imparted its own distinctive coloration to western morality for two millennia; its spokesmen have not hesitated to adopt a didactic idiom on every conceivable subject. It would be pleasant to report that imaginative literature has been viewed as a parallel spiritual enterprise, conducted under different auspices perhaps, obedient to its own logic certainly, but still capable of providing the kind of nourishment the ethical life needs if it is to emerge into the light. The reality, however, is quite different: the imagination and its works are patronised, or bullied into conformity with some pre-existing moral scheme, or degraded to the merely decorative, or, occasionally, plundered for moral *sententiae*. Worse still, imagination is sometimes seen as suspect. St Paul tells us in a famous passage that when he became a man he put behind him childish things; the Vulgate reads: '*evacuavi quae erant parvuli*',[5] with the verb '*evacuavi*' indicating a particularly emphatic repudiation. I cite the phrase in the form Augustine knew and possibly had in mind when he rounded on his earlier self, the young Augustine who read Virgil passionately and was moved to tears by the death of Dido. This episode in *The Confessions* is instructive because the language used by the mature Augustine testifies to the continuing presence of the poetry in his heart of hearts. The very phrase he uses when condemning his misplaced youthful sympathy for the tragic queen who committed suicide when abandoned by her lover has an almost Virgilian cadence: '*plorare Didonem mortuam*' (to weep at Dido's death).[6] But here, in his own words, Augustine tells against himself, the surest index of his greatness as a writer; the tension between the official moralist and the unofficial imaginative writer who cannot but renew and relive his poetic response makes the passage unforgettable. On the other hand, Newman, who like Augustine memorised Virgil in his young days, is quite unembarrassed in recalling the poetry that moved him and helped to form his tragic sense of life. In a haunting passage in *The Grammar of Assent* he marvels at how lines which are 'the birth of some chance morning or evening at an Ionian festival, or among the Sabine hills'[7] live in the grateful memory of generations of readers. He goes on to speculate that the reverence paid to Virgil in medieval Europe owed much to the paradoxical combination of power and charm in his verse: 'Perhaps this is the reason of the medieval opinion about Virgil, as if a prophet or magician; his single words and phrases, his pathetic half-lines, giving utterance, as the voice of nature herself, to the pain and weariness, yet hope of better things, which is the experience of her children in every time.'[8]

That wonderful passage, as humble as it is perceptive, expresses the purest gratitude for a literary experience which has entered into and formed Newman's sensibility. But he failed to infect his own commentators with a liking for poetry. Even Thomas Wall, while acknowledging the poetic strain audible everywhere in Newman's prose and occasionally even in his verse, cannot resist the temptation to put poetry in its proper and subordinate place: 'Poetry is perhaps best in the background, most comely in her handmaid's robes, with at least the hint of a blush – the dawning purple – on her cheeks. Too forward and gaudily attired, crowned with baleful splendours, she is something of a Jezebel and her

song is the song of a siren.'[9] Those who are offended by the blatantly
sexist language of condescension in that passage might exercise themselves on an earlier pronouncement in the same essay: 'Poetry, generally
represented as female, may sometimes be a vixen.'[10] But there is a more
depressing feature of this highly figurative prose than its sexism. The
elaborate and ostentatious imagery is intended to convey the idea that
the author, if so moved, could quite easily and successfully deviate into
poetry. Happily for us, however, Wall was preoccupied with what he
took to be more important and ponderous matters. I cite him because
the uncomprehending disciple, not the accomplished master, seems to
have determined the 'official' church's attitude to literature and the arts
in general; it might be characterised as vaguely supportive in a conde-
scending way, as if to make clear that no instruction and no formation
could be received from imaginative literature not readily available elsewhere. You may guess where.

Yet some of the doctrine and dogmas of the Catholic Church are
pure poetry: the Resurrection of the Body, the Communion of Saints,
the Mystical Body, the Assumption – not the doctrines on which
homilists choose to enlighten us these days. And it's not so long ago that
the splendours of Catholic liturgy ravished the eyes and ears of the
devout. The spiritual life of the faithful was nourished by prayers of
quite extraordinary intensity and beauty. Nowadays the only registers of
language which are permitted in addressing the deity are the conversa-
tional and the epistolary. But enough of this middle-aged nostalgia!

III

What then are the texts which address our beleaguered condition most
directly and yet permit us to live in hope of better things? Stewart
Parker's *Pentecost* comes immediately to mind, largely because of the
exquisitely sensitive and deeply moving production, directed by the
playwright's niece, Lynne Parker, currently playing in the Project
Theatre to packed and extraordinarily receptive houses.[11] But the play
has been a warm and vivid presence with me since I saw the original
production, directed by Patrick Mason, in 1987, the year before Stewart
Parker's tragically premature death. I should add that my sense of the
play has been coloured by conversation with Mary Holland and by the
characteristically generous and brilliantly perceptive critique she wrote in
a column for the *Irish Times*, 'Tongues of Fire where Hope and History
Rhyme',[12] a title which conflates the visionary aspect of Parker's play

with a celebrated line from Seamus Heaney's *The Cure at Troy*, his version of the *Philoctetes* of Sophocles.

And yet the first and most important point to make about *Pentecost* is that it functions almost entirely on the level of prosaic realism, which is where we live most of the time. It is, of course, a realism laced with wicked wit of the kind we might expect from the author of that mortuary comedy, *Nightshade*. Lynne Parker's production is as naturalistic as the acting area in the Project permits. It is played virtually in the round with the audience seated on three sides of the stage which represents, with almost pedantic attention to detail, the living-room of a terraced house on the Peace Line between Protestant and Catholic communities in Belfast. The gestures and movements of the actors are so carefully plotted that we come to know the domestic geography of the whole house and can surmise readily the political geography of the surrounding streets. The time is 1974; the strike organised by the Ulster Worker's Council to bring down the power-sharing executive in Stormont is in progress. The British government is engaged in one of its routine exercises of self-righteousness as an alternative to the enforcement of the rule of law. The extreme fragility of the social contract on which both Catholic and Protestants depend for the necessities of life is cruelly exposed. The four principals, an estranged Catholic couple thrown together again quite fortuitously, and two Protestant friends who join them under circumstantial but entirely plausible pressures all live in the beleaguered house on the razor's edge. Not surprisingly, they grate on each other's nerves. The play is remarkable for its scrupulous notation of Belfast speech and mores, for the exactness with which it discriminates between Catholic and Protestant imagery, idioms, iconographies and cultures, while still contriving to suggest that the mutual intelligibility of the characters, and especially their capacity to insult and wound each other in the ferocious quarrels with which the course of the action is punctuated, makes them also members of some larger, more inclusive, if as yet only dimly realised community of interest and affection.

But the naturalism of *Pentecost*, which renders the very texture of Belfast life with such delighted intimacy and exasperated inwardness, is hospitable to kinds of awareness not usually vouchsafed in the most familiar and banal, though by no means exhausted, of theatrical conventions. This is partly a function of the sheer intensity of Parker's writing and the acting of the Rough Magic company, in particular of Eleanor Methven whose performance in the role of Marian is incandescent. But it has even more to do with the playwright's stubborn, incorrigible optimism about human beings who are never complete in themselves, and not quite identical with themselves from moment to moment, either. The many terrible things said and done in this play are first owned by the characters and then, tentatively and rather shamefacedly, recognised for the spiteful and malignant things they are, before being disowned. Gradually, almost imperceptibly, the naturalism of *Pentecost* becomes porous, though it is never quite abandoned, as Parker seeks a theatrical embodiment of what his characters desire but cannot admit, what their actuality denies them but cannot quite destroy. The first intimation of other modes of being than those sanctioned by pure naturalism comes from the appearance of the ghost of Lily Matthews, the severely Presbyterian widow and lately deceased inhabitant of the terraced house, early in the second scene. By the last of the play's five scenes, when each of the characters in turn, moved by thoughts beyond the reaches of their souls, is beginning to speak with tongues of fire, Lily is redundant; her ghost vanishes and it is left to Marian to tell her tragic story. Parker is at pains to ensure that these ghostly apparitions do not constitute a gross violation of the play's naturalism; Lily is perfectly at home, posthumously, on the stage. She is visible and audible only to Marian, an antique dealer by trade who is a connoisseur of those objects which are eloquent of lives of quiet desperation, lived anonymously, unregarded by history. She studies the documents Lily left behind her and discovers a mildewed diary miserably eloquent of an unspoken, slow-motion, lifelong tragedy. Lily's ghost is the speaking likeness Marian constructs from her literary remains, if we can call them such; there is nothing spooky or melodramatic about her appearances. When we see her first, she is wearing her good Sunday coat and hat and carrying a bag; later she wears the print dress gifted to her by the lover who fathered the baby she abandoned in fear of her jealous and impotent husband's rage. So this ghost is matter-of-fact, homespun, demotic in speech, as perversely proud and savagely respectable in death as in life. But Parker is too good a dramatist to fix her in a purely retrospective posture; Lily's ghost is no pillar of salt focused exclusively on the past. She lives as a character in the vivid present tense of her anti-Catholic bigotry; her sense of Marian's religious affiliation is purely olfactory, a matter of smelling out the old enemy's incense. Lily is the embittered, reluctant host whose Catholic and Protestant guests evince, in spite of themselves, similar or opposing prejudices almost as deeply ingrained as her own.

There could hardly be a more unpromising setting for the expression of hope. Yet this is precisely what happens in the last scene of *Pentecost:* the characters, each after his or her fashion, gesture towards a future which is not simply an extension of the past. Even here, the orchestration of their voices is suggestive of a discordant symphony, at least until Marian gathers all the timid hopes of her friends into her opulent, yet piercing and painful final speeches. Mary Holland rightly remarked on the difficulty of receiving in 1987 that strenuous expression of hope against hope,[13] when hope itself, given the conditions actually prevailing in Northern Ireland, seemed too much to hope for, seemed more like a self-inflicted wound on tender sensibilities, better hardened and toughened against such weakness. She is, of course, right to underline the fact that we respond to *Pentecost* differently now, but she rather underestimates the sense of difficulties being overcome in that still withering and punishing final scene. There is nothing facile about Marian's final speech; her syntax suffers what an engineer would call plastic deformation, and is strained almost to breaking point. Besides, Parker works through blasphemy and bigotry, through tense and odious confessions, through violence and grotesque comedy, before Marian can voice the Christian hope in terms which makes a new beginning imaginable and possible for all four tormented, temporary residents in Lily's haunted house. And the audience is not allowed to lose sight of the fact that counterpointing the *Sursum Corda* movement in Marian's final aria is the ugly triumphalism of the rampant Protestant strikers at the collapse of the power-sharing executive.

The unpredictable and extravagant movement of the last scene in *Pentecost* only becomes possible when Marian allows herself to remember the baby Christopher she bore Lenny in August 1969, at the beginning of the Troubles. She acknowledges the bitterness she felt at his death a mere five months later, a bitterness she has jealously hoarded ever since, to the point where it has poisoned her. Remembering Christopher she confesses: 'I denied him. The Christ in him. Which He had entrusted to my care, the ghost of him that I do still carry, as I carried his little body. The Christ in him absorbed into the Christ in me. We have got to love that in ourselves. In ourselves first and then in them. That's the only future there is.'[14] A moment later she declares: 'Personally, I want to live now. I want this house to live. We have committed sacrilege enough, in this place, in this time. We don't owe it to ourselves, we owe it to our dead ... our innocent dead. They're not our masters, they're only our creditors, for the life they never knew. We owe them at least that – the fullest life for which they could ever have hoped, we carry those ghosts within us, to betray those hopes is the real sin against the Christ, and I for one cannot commit it one day longer.'[15]

Her friends, already emotionally devastated, grope towards a gesture somehow not inadequate to the surge of feeling they experience; we sense their pain, as of blood returning to a limb from which it has been drained by violent exertion. Marian's Protestant friend, Ruth, reads from Lily's Bible, that passage in the Acts of the Apostles beginning: 'Therefore shall my soul rejoice ...' No breach of decorum is involved here, however, for Ruth has earlier quoted verbatim from the same text the account of the first Pentecost, admittedly with occasional promptings from her lover Peter. Lenny, Marian's husband, moved beyond words by her articulation of what is also his pain and his desire, takes his trusty trombone with him into the yard, sits on the window ledge and plays a deliciously lugubrious, bluesy version of 'Just a Closer Walk with Thee' which Peter, not to be outdone, picks out on his banjo in an almost comically inadequate accompaniment.

It is precisely because these hesitant, tentative, faltering expressions, whether verbal or musical, are so completely free from any hint of inhibiting or paralysing embarrassment that we come at the end of *Pentecost* to the heights of tragedy. Perhaps the final chorus in Milton's *Samson Agonistes* defines the mood of the audience issuing from the Project most accurately:

> His servants he with new acquist
> Of true experience from this great event
> With peace and consolation hath dismist,
> And calm of mind all passions spent.

There is, of course, no ethical prescription in *Pentecost*, though no audience which lives through the drama can fail to glimpse new, as yet undreamt-of possibilities, political, social and moral. It is a fortifying play.

But I am nothing if not critical and I propose now a limiting judgement. It is clear from the first moment of *Pentecost* to its last gasp of hope, that Parker could not have written his play without a completely absorbing and potentially dangerous engagement with Eugene O'Neill's *Long Day's Journey into Night*. The resemblances are too striking and too numerous to be accidental. Both plays use naturalistic conventions and transcend them, without violating them. The dramatic conflicts are represented initially in terms of character, but increasingly in terms of competing and apparently irreconcilable narratives; the drama in the final scenes of both plays resides in the clash of narratives, which rebuke, contradict and correct each other until a final inclusive story, at once prospective and retrospective, is arrived at. In both *Pentecost* and *Long Day's Journey into Night* the leading female character is groping towards a specifically Christian faith at the final curtain. Both plays are torrential in their verbosity but issue finally in wordlessness; it might not be entirely frivolous to suggest that Lenny's trombone is the musical equivalent of O'Neill's melancholy foghorn, or that Peter's pathetic picking on the banjo is a phantom reminiscence of Mary Tyrone's brittle piano-playing. Both plays end with dawn breaking and four characters waiting to receive a grace which may (or may not) be granted. Neither play pretends that the old Adam, locked up securely in the bosom of each character, can be extirpated in favour of some superior and more radiant being; both plays insist that there is no alternative to an unqualified love of ourselves and others, as we are, without bitterness or rancour but in full consciousness of our insufficiency. The characters are seen finally in the light of a transfiguration; we are not required to believe in their transformation out of all recognition.

It is arguable that *Pentecost* benefited from its great precursor in an even more important and fundamental way. Mary Holland characterises Parker's own Christianity as 'rooted deeply in the Protestant evangelical tradition, believing in the possibility of individual salvation through Christ.'[16] He might have written a compelling, though not, I think, a tragic drama in terms entirely consonant with that tradition. But *Pentecost* is not a study of individual agony or redemption; the four principals, however much at odds with each other they are, constitute a group, a social microcosm which is more than the aggregate of the individuals who comprise it. The same can be said for the Tyrone family in *Long Day's Journey into Night*. Parker's group and O'Neill's family are both fissiparous, though both are intact at the end of their respective plays, no one can say for how long. Drama is a social art, the most social of the arts, whether you think in terms of the occasion of its performance before an audience which collaborates with it or in terms of the experiences it renders and makes available. The movements of Marian's mind, her complications of thought and feeling, given in the speeches I quoted earlier, have social reverberations and social consequences; they impact on others and are amplified in the responses of the on-stage audience. This is precisely why they acquire a kind of tragic force. The immensely moving power of *Pentecost* must owe something, if not everything, to *Long Day's Journey into Night*.

Parker's play certainly invites comparison with O'Neill's and, as we have seen, is not humiliated in the process. If *Long Day's Journey into Night* emerges as the better play, this is not a black mark against *Pentecost* for O'Neill's masterpiece is one of perhaps the five or six greatest plays of the twentieth century; only *Uncle Vanya*, *The Playboy of the Western World, The Plough and the Stars, The Crucible* and *Waiting for Godot* can live long with it. But there is, I think, something too declamatory, too self-consciously hortatory in Marian's final speeches. Parker's attempt to generalise the house and its beleaguered little group into a symbolic equivalent of the larger community is too explicit and too emphatic for comfort; he is betrayed into doing the audience's work for it, as if his confidence in the power of his play to command the response he craved had momentarily failed. The upbeat ending of *Pentecost* is a shade too insistent, the contrast with *Long Day's Journey into Night* almost too cruel. You may also experience a twinge or scruple of doubt about Marian's declaration that we must love the Christ in ourselves before we can find and love him in others, as if Christ could be know in a social vacuum, and as if the self could be known before the other.

IV

For some time now, Michael Longley has been adapting Homer, carving out of *The Iliad* and *The Odyssey* perfect gemlike lyrics. The impulse behind this project is not archaeological or scholarly, but creative. Longley's fidelity as a poet is not paid exclusively to Homer whom he respects above all others; the Homeric sequence represents his oblique but intense response to the urgencies of the writing moment in which he finds himself besieged by political imperatives and humane revulsion at appalling acts of violence. Not that he editorialises on the relevance of his poems; he is far too conscientious an artist to engage in such pomposity. In reimagining Homeric scenes as clearly and vividly as he can, Longley is instructed by his own experience, literary and extra-literary; the informing rhythms are those of contemporary speech; the diction is increasingly coloured and diversified by dialect words and contemporary cultural references. A few lines from 'The Butchers', the last poem in *Gorse Fields*, will illustrate the power of the poetry. Odysseus, his long wanderings after the fall of Troy now over and the sailors who paid court to Penelope all despatched, attends with his son Telemachos to some unfinished business.

> Odysseus, spattered with muck and like a lion dripping with blood
> From his chest and cheeks after devouring a farmer's
>   bullock,
> Ordered the disloyal housemaids to sponge down the
>   armchairs

And tables, while Telemachos, the oxherd and the
   swineherd
Scraped the floor with shovels, and then between the
   portico
And the roundhouse stretched a hawser and hanged the women
So none touched the ground with her toes, like
   long-winged thrushes
Or doves trapped in a mist-net across the thicket where they roost
Their heads bobbing in a row, their feet twitching but not for
   long.
And when they dragged Melanchios's corpse into the
   haggard,
And cut off his nose and ears and cock and balls, a dog's dinner,
Odysseus, seeing the need for whitewash and disinfectant,
Fumigated the house and the outhouses, so that Hermes
Like a clergyman might wave the supernatural baton
With which he resurrects or hypnotises those he chooses ...'[7]

It is a perfectly appalling scene, the horror of which is unmitigated by
any softening or moralising commentary. But it is also a scene which
cannot be kept at arms' length or relegated to a barbaric past. The diction does not permit the reader to engage in such an act of distanciation:
words like 'muck', 'armchairs', 'roadhouse', 'haggard', 'cock', 'balls' and
'disinfectant', not to speak of 'clergyman', have too salient a currency.

But, as many of you will have guessed, the poem of Longley's on
which I want to dwell is 'Ceasefire', first published in the *Irish Times* in
a quite uncanny coincidence with the IRA's announcement of its ceasefire. Uncanny, and yet the process is familiar enough. How often has it
happened that a poet, consulting his own deep imaginative impulses and
abandoning himself to the creative task those very impulses enjoin him,
has articulated not only his own concerns but those of the moment or
the moment to be that is not yet fully formed. Of course, this only happens when a poet makes an act of complete confidence in the imagination and has the necessary resources of courage, skill and daring to take
the risks attendant on the creative act. To the receptive reader it is as if
the poet has acquired incredibly sensitive and subtle antennae.

Ceasefire

I

Put in mind of his own father and moved to tears
Achilles took him by the hand and pushed the old king
Gently away, but Priam curled up at his feet and
Wept with him until their sadness filled the building.

II

Taking Hector's corpse into his own hands Achilles
Made sure it was washed and, for the old King's sake,
Laid out in uniform, ready for Priam to carry
Wrapped like a present home to Troy at daybreak

III

When they had eaten together, it pleased them both
To stare at each other's beauty as lovers might,
Achilles built like a god, Priam good-looking still
And full of conversation, who earlier had sighed:

IV

'I get down on my knees and do what must be done
And kiss Achilles' hand, the killer of my son.'[18]

The form in which Longley casts this famous incident is of crucial
importance. 'Ceasefire' is an adaptation of the Shakespearean sonnet in
three quatrains, rhyming the second and fourth line ending, either
imperfectly as with 'might ' and 'sighed' in the third quatrain, or with a
heavily stressed monosyllable rhyming with the lightly stressed last sylla-
ble in a disyllabic work (thus 'king' rhymes with the '...ing' of 'building'
and 'sake' with the '...break' of 'daybreak'). The other, half-expected
rhymes do not occur. In the final couplet the monosyllabic verb 'done'
rhymes with the monosyllabic noun 'son', the only perfect rhyme in the
whole poem, one for which we are forced to wait anxiously.

Structurally, too, the poem is full of tiny surprises. The grief of
Priam and the more unexpected grief of Achilles, moved by the recollection of his own father, is strongly stated in the first quatrain where the
word 'gently', is both surprising and enormously suggestive. The second
quatrain, in which Achilles himself performs the ritual ablution of
Hector's body, is rather more surprising: a great hero performs a menial

task but is not demeaned. The third quatrain is almost shocking in its unexpectedness, as bereaved father and son-killer, having dined together, enjoy with notable frankness each other's physical presence and find each other's company congenial. And then, in the final couplet, almost by way of afterthought, comes Priam's recollection of what he had earlier said to himself and done: a perfect rhyming, so to speak, not only of word and word but of word and deed.

> 'I get down on my knees and do what must be done
> And kiss Achilles' hand, the killer of my son.'

This is the only occurrence of direct speech in the poem; these are the only verbs in the present tense. And yet they refer to that which has already been done; without losing their prophetic power.

The whole poem seems on inspection to be very close to reportage, yet it is at the same time an obviously prophetic utterance in a cooler idiom than Marian's speeches at the end of *Pentecost* but as vibrant with emotion and desire. It is also qualified by the same kind of cruel irony which sounds as a kind of bass note to Marian's prophetic carolling in *Pentecost*. This moving incident was merely an episode in the Trojan war; Troy was doomed to fall anyway, no matter what Priam and Achilles said and did. No matter what accommodation they might have reached with each other and confirmed with bloody hands. Similarly, when Parker was writing *Pentecost* in the mid-eighties and casting his mind back on the events of 1974, he was conscious, and expected his audience to be conscious, of all that had happened in the intervening years. Yet Priam's words (and Marian's) are not drained of meaning and value; neither do they lose their exemplary quality.

At this point it is surely time for a change of key. *Pentecost* makes us keenly aware both of how delicate the social fabric is and of how desperately important it is to maintain it, if we are to have a truly human life, indeed any kind of life at all. The epigraph of Michael O'Siadhail's recent collection, *A Fragile City*, is taken from the old Greek philosopher Epictetus who in a moment of blinding insight identified the '*polis*', that is the community or city, with the cosmos, the whole universe of things, an almost Pauline image. The final sequence in *A Fragile City* is called 'Feast' and contains a dozen poems of pure celebration. For O'Siadhail, the occasions which call for celebration are at once given gratuitously and answered freely, products of grace abounding and of grave civility and courtesy. The poem 'Abundance' emphasises the givenness of such moments in the idiom of pure gratitude. It begins:

To be there, childlike, when it happens.
Nothing I've ever earned or achieved.
Delight. Sudden quivers of abundance.
A whole glorious day with a friend.
Brunch. This honeyed break. Talk.
All the time in the world to spend.[19]

Every single one of these nine sentences, two of them mere monosyllabic words, is cheated of its finite verb as if to signal the astonishment of the
imagination overpowered by the unreasonable abundance of life which at
its best makes no economic sense. But these words do something more
than entertain the idea of celebration; they create a sort of charmed space,
invitingly open to the reader whose communion with the hospitable spirit
of the poem also becomes a celebration. The last line of the poem stands
alone – the rest is in tightly grouped and rhymed tercets – but not as a
forbidding sentinel, rather as an expression of wonder common to speaker
and reader: 'so much is that might never have been.' In 'Michaelmas at
Glendalough' O'Siadhail celebrates a lost, beautiful harmony of Christianity
with the sensuous richness of the natural world.

Clusters of monks gathered in a first
Burgeoning, that strange lyrical outburst
Of separate worlds just newly spliced:
The lush blackbird, the eastern Christ.[20]

But O'Siadhail also celebrates the rich human courtesies, elaborately
formal and decorous, yet warmly hospitable. In 'Delight' he imagines a
meal, almost drooling with lascivious pleasure in food, but taking delight
in the delight of others, as a host should.

Let the meal be simple. A big plate
of mussels, warm bread with garlic,
and enough mulled wine to celebrate

Being here, I open a hinged mussel
piercing a balloon of plump meat
from the blue wings of a shell.

A table's rising decibels of fun.
Such gossip. A story caps a story.
Banter. Then, another pun on a pun.[21]

Perhaps the most beautiful instance of that hospitable impulse which is the best, the most human and the most divine of human attributes, comes in the poem called, appropriately enough, 'Courtesy'. O'Siadhail recalls an incident from the early days of space travel when a group of astronauts departing from a space station remembered those who would replace them.

> The Russian astronauts leaving after them
> Bread and salt for the next to dock
> At the station. Small symbols of welcome.[22]

That whole poem is animated by the sense that in those moments when we receive each other with grace, we are not just hosts to guests in our houses, not just members of the polis, not only citizens of the universe (in Epictetus' wonderful conceit) but 'citizens of paradise', as O'Siadhail puts it. At the end of 'Courtesy' something remarkable happens: the speaker in the poem, while remaining in place as the dutiful host surrounded by guests on a convivial occasion, permits the poet to look out at his own readers, invitingly.

> I feed on such courtesy.
> These guests keep countenancing me.
> Mine always mine. This complicity
> Of faces, companions, breadbreakers.
> You and you and you. My fragile city.[23]

O'Siadhail's poems are written in the optative mood, giving shape and form to our desire, and are themselves contrived to produce in words the very occasions they celebrate so intensely. He gives us our just desserts, if you can find it in your heart to forgive the pun; his poems are instances of the courtesy they celebrate.

V

I will conclude with some reflections on a very different work, Eoin McNamee's remarkable novel *Resurrection Man*, published last year and almost immediately remaindered, more because of the distasteful nature of its subject, I fancy, than for any weaknesses or failings on the author's part. In fact, no novel I have read in recent years has anything like the sustained intensity, the graphic realism, the utter credibility or the disciplined precision of *Resurrection Man*, in comparison with which even John Banville's chilling novel, *The Book of Evidence*, seems almost genial. McNamee's novel is based on Martin Dillon's painstaking study of the career of the Shankill Butchers which was first published in 1989.[24] There is little need to remind you of the facts. The Shankill Butchers were an almost impenetrable cell of Protestant paramilitaries active in the 1970s who tortured, brutalised and murdered Catholics chosen at random with the inevitable result that some of their thirty-odd victims were of their own persuasion. The evil genius who presided over them, manipulating them even when he was incarcerated in Crumlin Road jail was born Hugh Leonard Thompson ('Lenny) Murphy on 2 March 1952 and was shot to pieces early in the evening of 16 November 1982 in what appears to have been a joint operation by the IRA and loyalist paramilitaries with the latter 'fingering' Murphy for the former. For all his comparative youth Lenny Murphy was no novice in evil, though he was never actually charged with murder. The confessions of his associates, who refrained from naming him during his lifetime, make it clear that he terrorised them as much as the Catholic community on which he preyed. It is clear that Murphy was a loner of a quite extreme kind; the illusion of self-sufficiency with which he vested himself must have contributed significantly to his leadership mystique. Dillon is greatly exercised in the course of his book to understand the evil of Lenny Murphy and his group. He adduces the heightened prejudice and mutual suspicion of the two Northern communities. He instances the effect of Murphy's Catholic name on his psyche; Lenny was nicknamed 'Mick' by Protestant companions at school and recoiled violently from the suggested identification with the hated Catholics. Dillon also notes that the trial judge, who handed down forty-two life sentences in a single sitting when a number of Murphy's associates were convicted of multiple murder, accepted the psychiatrist's conclusion that they were not suffering from 'any diagnosable mental illness' and indicates his belief that a similar conclusion would have been arrived at by any psychiatrist deputed to examine Murphy himself.[25]

Although Dillon's study of the Shankill Butchers has considerable explanatory power in detailing the circumstances which enabled the butchers to realise their full murderous potential, he cannot be said to have explained the evil itself in its pure, concentrated form. This black hole in the heart of *The Shankill Butchers* is quite possibly what stimulated Eoin McNamee's interest in the subject. There is a passage in one of the butchers' confessions which may explain the very deliberate choice of style adopted in the novel. Kenneth McClinton murdered a

Protestant bus driver who broke the strike organised by the Workers' Council in 1976 in imitation of the successful one in 1974 which frames the action of *Pentecost*. In common with other Protestant paramilitaries, McClinton experienced something of a religious conversion in jail. But it is the terms he used to describe the reaction of the bus driver to the impact of the bullet fired at point blank into his head which I want to consider. 'It was just like that shooting which they have shown on television, the famous one where a South Vietnamese army officer shoots this member of the Viet Cong on the street in Saigon. The blood spurted out of his head. Shooting the bus driver was just like that. I could see it all in colour. It was just like I saw it in that television report ... it was like you would see it in a film.'[26] What you have at work here is a low-voltage imagination engaged in the aestheticization and trivialization of its own violence according to a cultural pattern which is well established and understood, one which McClinton knows is second nature to his interrogator as well as to himself. The appeal he makes in terms of common understanding is obvious: it is implied in the word 'famous' – as if to say 'You know it well, don't you?' – and it is quite explicit in the final phrase: 'it was like you would see it in a film.' There is even a hint of self-satisfaction in McClinton's declaration: 'I could see it all in colour', the original film clip from the Vietnam War was in black-and-white.

Eoin McNamee writes with a mind of winter in a style drained completely of all colours, a style without flourishes of any kind, as lapidary as that of a stone-mason. He is concerned with 'the raw, untransformed facts of the Resurrection Men'[27] before their harsh contours yield to what is called in the same passage 'the adaptable myths of television' or the older seductions of urban folklore, never mind the blizzard of verbal clichès in contemporary newspaper reports. I mention the latter because Coppinger and Ryan, two important characters in *Resurrection Man*, are journalists conscious of handling events which are beyond the normal reach of their trade. The central figure is Victor Kelly (McNamee's version of Lenny Murphy), a serial killer with an ideological 'justification' as well as a terrible inner need or compulsion: but he is no psychopath. His killings are negative analogues for the processes of creation. His mind is an inexhaustible repertoire of film sequences, like the one which McClinton recalled in the extract from *The Shankill Butchers* I quoted a few moments ago. But if Kelly aestheticizes violence, the novel emphatically does not. McNamee's achievement is to make us horribly familiar with, even intimate with violence; *Resurrection Man* enables us to feel 'the fascination of evil', but at one remove, as if in the polished mirror of the shield with which Perseus confronted the Gorgon.

John Banville's slightly earlier novel *The Book of Evidence* is interested in very similar, closely adjacent psychic territory, though it differs from McNamee's novel in a number of important respects, technically, stylistically and, most significantly, in terms of perspective. But a brief comparison of the two novels may be useful. It is notable, for instance, that Banville through his first-person narrator Freddie Montgomery, another murderer, gives far more explicit signposts as to the nature of the state of mind he is interested in exploring. At one point Freddie, incarcerated in Mountjoy, tells his defence council that it is pointless to search for mitigating circumstances: 'I meant to kill her. You know ... I have no explanation, and no excuse.'[28] But a little later he goes further: 'This is the worst, the essential sin I think, for which there will be no forgiveness: that I never imagined her sufficiently, that I did not make her live. Yes, that failure of imagination is my real crime, the one that made the others possible. What I told that policeman is true – I killed her because I could kill her, and I could kill her because for me she was not alive.'[29] There are profound truths about evil here which do not palliate its horror or diminish its mystery.

But there are problems with *The Book of Evidence* which do not afflict *Resurrection Man*, though they are the direct result of very deliberate compositional choices, choices which help to make it the supremely sophisticated, glittering masterpiece it is while in the last analysis requiring a qualified judgement. My scruples are agitated by the use of a first-person narrator which has the effect of creating an irrefragable bond with the reader and of generating willy-nilly an unearned, and by no means purely imaginative sympathy with Freddie Montgomery. What is given spontaneously by the reader cannot easily be withdrawn – it is proof against irony even of the subtlest kind. It is right and proper that we should be complicit with Freddie Montgomery, made intimate partakers in the evil he represents; much less welcome is the confusion of our aesthetic, moral and emotional response. Even in the wonderful and harrowing passages just quoted, the insistent 'I' of Freddie Montgomery acquires a certain glamour, a kind of gloss or patina, which suggests a certain smugness utterly at odds with the speaker's wish to attest to the human reality of his victim. Josie Bell simply doesn't have the same ontological status as Freddie Montgomery either for Freddie himself or for the reader. Finally, and this too is a function of Banville's narrative perspective, the dominant, mandarin style of the narrator and the novel, the highly mannered and exquisitely cadenced prose with its dazzling range of reference and allusion, is so far at odds with the squalor and brutality of the crime that is the engine of the narrative, that the evil is muffled and cushioned to some extent. Banville, of course, knows exactly what he is doing and *The Book of Evidence* has a multiplicity of concerns quite different from those being considered at the moment. Nevertheless, in fiction self-consciousness and knowingness, though absolutely indispensable, are not of themselves enough.

The point of this brief excursion into comparative criticism is to suggest that *Resurrection Man* is not vulnerable on these grounds; its effect is not blurred or blunted, though long before the end we might wish it had been. I borrowed a famous phrase from Wallace Stevens ('A mind of winter') to indicate McNamee's attitude to his subject. *Resurrection Man* is a novel of sustained, unremitting intensity and severity which supplies an objective correlative for evil. With Freddie Montgomery's characteristically self-regarding voice still in your mind, attend to this passage from early in *Resurrection Man* ...

Victor Kelly is sitting at the wheel of a Ford Zephyr abandoned on the docks at the centre of Belfast; as night thickens about him he conjures with his immediate sensations, with images of the city which comes into its own with darkness and with memories of Hollywood films:

> Victor sat at the wheel of the car until dusk most nights. He preferred it when it began to get dark. By day the city seemed ancient and ambiguous. Its power was dissipated by exposure to daylight. It looked derelict and colonial. There was a sense of curfew, of produce rotting in the market place. At night it described itself by its lights, defining streets like a code of destinations. Victor would sit with the big wheel of the Zephyr pressed against his chest and think about John Dillinger's face seen through a windscreen at night, looking pinched by rain and the deceit of women.[30]

This is remarkable, disciplined writing, though it is emphatically not the kind of prose to which anthologies are hospitable. There is no hint of purple in the deliberate syntactical banalities, the heavy reliance on the treacherous pronoun 'it', the conscious avoidance of irony. Nevertheless, it is simultaneously a subtle example of the scene-agent ratio in fiction, operating almost mid-way between metaphor and metonymy, with an insight almost uncanny. This is a style which calls no attention to itself, being utterly engrossed in what is placed squarely before it; it characterises Victor Kelly with a degree of inwardness and precision which is both utterly convincing and alarming. You will have noticed the geometrical quality of the word 'described'; the 'destinations' it proposes, in a code perfectly legible to Victor who knows the political geography of the city are purely internal. We might want to read the passage as a poetic metaphor for the mind of the protagonist, or as a prosaic metonymy with Victor held in loose suspension with Belfast. But the prose seems to me to prevent us from making either of these familiar moves with any degree of comfort. The moral reality of this monster is both utterly convincing and quite simply incapable of assimilation or appropriation in those ways: he never loses his strangeness, though he becomes our familiar.

I do not propose to go into detail about Victor's murderous career, though I would remark on the combination of clarity and chastity in the writing, another paradoxical feature of the book. But I want to cite two other passages which communicate the peculiar flavour of the novel. Quite late in the book Victor confides in his girlfriend Heather; it is important to note that McNamee uses cursory reported speech.

> He said little about the killings themselves but he managed to convey the impression of something deft and surgical achieved at the outer limits of necessity, cast beyond the range of the spoken word where the victim was cherished and his killers attentive to some terrible need that he carried with him. Victor used the victim's full names. He told her how he found himself in sympathy with their faults and hinted that during their last journey he nursed them towards a growing awareness of their wasted years and arranged their bodies finally with an eye to the decorous and eternal.
> Kill me.[31]

It is Victor who aestheticizes violence here, who claims a particular intimacy with his victims, performing for them what is virtually a priest-like task. The final phrase, 'Kill me', echoes through the whole novel; it is the cry for mercy uttered repeatedly by the recipients of Victor's ministrations. Whether it is here to be construed as part of Victor's 'confession' to Heather, or as something unspoken which she intuits, is undecidable, deliberately so.

Finally, I want to attend to the account given in *Resurrection Man* of Victor's own death. He emerges from his mother's house (unlike Lenny Murphy who was shot outside his girlfriend's flat) to discover that he has been abandoned by his associate McClure.

Then he realised that McClure wasn't there and he felt an expression cross his face like a film, something's wrong. His eyes searched the street and somehow he knew that it was a fateful wrong. He shaded his eyes and looked into the momentous dark. It was hard to see. He needed light, any light and there it was suddenly above him. A sniper's lonely moon. He saw the three men getting out of the back of the Commer van, running, carrying rifles held across their chests. He saw them take cover behind parked cars, raise the rifles into firing position. Victor never thought it would be like this, time going by with deadly ease. He pulled the Browning out from under his jacket and looked for cover. But nothing was right. He wanted them to be serious-minded men who shouted out a warning. He wanted words full of allure and danger to shout back. Never take me alive. The rifle fire had a flat industrial sound. Victor felt the bullets force him back against the door. Victor knew the moves. Struggle to raise the gun. Clutch the breast and lean forward in anguish. His face hit the pavement. He did not see one of the men leave cover and walk over to him and put his foot on his neck and shoot him through the back of the head with a snub-nose revolver. There were no words, got him at last. No rueful gangster smile, goodbye world.[32]

There is something almost pathetic about the way Victor's death breaches his sense of decorum, that lethal aesthetic with which he regards his own victims. He knows from his study of gangster movies (the final sequence in Raoul Walsh's *White Heat* is, I think, present to this mind) what the required gestures and words are, though they elude him and in any case his assassins are not so well versed in these mysteries as he is. This is not the first time tonight that we have found a deliberate and yet apt incongruity between style and substance in recent Irish writing; indeed, the more intense the vision, the more strenuously paradoxical is the treatment.

VI

This brief essay gives only the barest indication of the richness of imaginative literature. The plays, poems and novels we have been considering are necessary to our psychic and social health, though they do not yield moral prescription, spiritual formulations or political solutions. It ought to be a truism that the full potential of a literary text is available only to those readers who respect its literary form; such patience is the beginning of wisdom.

I have made no mention of our most celebrated authors, not because I doubt their achievement but rather because there is a particular excitement in the process of discovery – in the shocked recognition a novel like *Resurrection Man* exacts, for example. But in any attempt at self-understanding or self-transcendence the poetry of Seamus Heaney and Derek Mahon, the fiction of John McGahern and Edna O'Brien and the plays of Brian Friel and Tom Murphy are quite simply indispensable. It would be shameful if this age proved to be, in Auden's words, 'So lacking in conviction/It cannot take pure fiction.'[33] The richer and more abundant life we crave is prefigured in works of art.

NOTES

1 *New York Review of Books*, vol. XLIII, no. 2, pp. 35-42.
2 See Enda McDonagh, 'Church Needs a Centre to Find Itself', *Irish Times*, 13 November 1995.
3 For the text of 'In Memory of W.B. Yeats' see *W.H. Auden: A Selection by the Author* (London, 1958), pp. 66-7.
4 *Aeneid*, Book II, l. 724.
5 See Ad Corinthos, 13, 11 in *Novum Testamentum Graece et Latine* (Rome, 1938).
6 For the Latin citation see *St Augustine's Confessions*, ed. W.H.D. Rouse (Cambridge, Mass., 1968), p. 38.
7 *An Essay in Aid of a Grammar of Assent* (New York, 1955), p. 79.
8 Ibid. Joyce remembered this passage in *A Portrait of the Artist as a Young Man*.
9 'The Writer and Preacher', in Michael Tierney (ed.), *A Tribute to Newman* (Dublin, 1945), p. 360.
10 Ibid., p. 349.
11 The text of the play is given in *Three Plays for Ireland* (London, 1989). Lynne Parker's production ran in the Project through October 1995.
12 The article was published in the *Irish Times* for 12 October 1995.
13 Ibid.
14 See *Three Plays for Ireland*, p. 207.
15 Ibid., p. 208.
16 'A Time when Hope and History Rhyme', the *Irish Times*, 12 October 1955.
17 Michael Longley, *Gorse Field* (London, 1991), p. 51.
18 *The Ghost Orchid* (London, 1995), p. 35. 'Ceasefire' is based on an incident in Book XXIV of Homer's *Iliad*; there are a number of deliberate alterations, all of them significant.

19 *A Fragile City* (Newcastle Upon Tyne, 1995), p. 61.
20 Ibid., p. 66.
21 Ibid., p. 72.
22 Ibid., p. 73.
23 Ibid., p. 74.
24 *The Shankill Butchers: A Case Study of Mass Murder* (London, 1989).
25 Ibid., p. 332.
26 Ibid., p. 208.
27 *Resurrection Man* (London, 1994), p. 191. See also p. 58.
28 *The Book of Evidence* (London, 1989), p. 210.
29 Ibid., p. 215.
30 *Resurrection Man*, p. 6.
31 Ibid., p. 174.
32 Ibid., pp. 229-30.
33 *W. H. Auden: A Selection by the Author*, p. 148.

Credits

The editors and contributors gratefully acknowledge reproduction permission granted: Cistercian Publications, for the quotation in Dr Kane's essay from Fr Michael Casey's translation of St Bernard of Clairvaux's *Apologia* in Bernard of Clairvaux, *Apologia to Abbot William of Thierry, Cistercians and Cluniacs,* Cistercian Fathers Series 1A (Kalamazoo, Michigan: Cistercian Publications); lines of Patrick Kavanagh's poetry in Sr Agnew's essay are reproduced by kind permission of the Trustees of Patrick Kavanagh, c/o Peter Fallon, literary agent, Loughcrew, Oldcastle, Co. Meath, Ireland; in Margaret Kelleher's essay extracts from Eavan Boland's *Selected Poems* (1989), *Outside History* (1990) and *In a Time of Violence* (1994) appear by kind permission of the author and Carcanet Press, from Paula Meehan's *The Man who was Marked by Winter* (1991) by kind permission of the author and The Gallery Press, and from Nuala Ní Dhomhnaill's *Rogha Dánta/Selected Poems* (1991) by kind permission of the author and Raven Arts Press. Eileen Kane's essay includes a quotation from Erwin Panofsky, *Abbot Suger on the Abbey Church of Saint-Denis and its Art Treasures* © 1946 by Erwin Panofsky; reprinted by permission of Princeton University Press; in John Devitt's essay thanks are due to the following publishers: Oberon Books for permission to quote extracts from Stewart Parker's *Pentecost*, Bloodaxe Books for permission to quote from Michael O'Siadhail's *A Fragile City*; Picador Books for permission to quote extracts from Eoin McNamee's *Resurrection Man*. Special thanks to Michael Longley for permission to quote 'Ceasefire' and 'The Butchers'.

CREDITS FOR ILLUSTRATIONS.

In Eileen Kane's essay: figs. 1 and 2 are courtesy the Museo del Prado, Madrid fig. 3 is Copyright IRPA-KIK Bruxelles; the original of fig. 4 is in the church of San Marco, Florence.

In Gesa Thiessen's essay, credits for illustrations are as follows: Georges Rouault, *Ecce Home*, 1938/39, © Staatsgalerie Stuttgart; Pablo Picasso, *Guernica*, 1937, Museo Nacional Centro de Arte Reina Sofia, Madrid, © Succession Picasso/DACS 1996; Barnett Newman, *Lema Sabachthani, The Stations of the Cross, Thirteenth Station*, 1965, the Robert and Jane Meyerhoff Collection, © 1996 Board of Trustees, National Gallery of Art, Washington; Harry Clarke, *The Angel of Peace and Hope*, 1919, Holy Trinity Church,